FIZ

and some Theatre Giants

By Eleanor Fazan

Cover credits:
Portrait of Eleanor Fazan by Don Backardi
Back cover photo by Rowland McMaster
Cover design by Stan Ruecker

Produced by:

FriesenPress
Suite 300 – 852 Fort Street
Victoria, BC, Canada V8W 1H8

www.friesenpress.com

Distributed to the trade by The Ingram Book Company

This book is dedicated to:
Stanley Myers
and also to our son Nicolas Myers
and his children Ellie and Anna Myers.

And my always grateful thanks to
Paul Almond, O.C.
Edgar de Bresson
Terence Blacker
Harry Hook
and above all to my sister
Juliet Fazan McMaster, without whom …

Table of Contents

PREFACE

This book has had a bumpy ride. I started writing in the 1980s, a time when my work as a choreographer and a director was taking me all over the world. Stirring up old memories in various bleak, foreign apartments was, I found, rather comforting. Also I had promised Lindsay Anderson that I would. He loved my stories, mostly I think because, as a director himself, the one person he never saw working was another director, and so they fascinated him. "You've got to write all this down," he'd say. "And tell the *truth*. Remember – it's not often heard."

And so I began, perhaps appropriately while directing John Mortimer's *When That I Was* in Ottawa in 1980. After some years and indeed many interruptions (I've always had to work hard) I got stuck. "You'd better show me what you've done," Lindsay said. And I did. He telephoned me the very next morning. "Some pieces made me laugh and cry at the same time. But it's no good. No one is going to be interested in *you* – it's the people you've worked with who are interesting. Start again, and keep yourself out of it as much as you can."

I took Lindsay's advice, and from then on wrote about one person, or one subject, at a time, sending the pieces to Lindsay for his approval and corrections. He never told me what I should write; but the chapters would be returned with remarks like "A bit of a mess," "Not a true picture," "Expand on this" – written in red ink. And that would spur me on.

Juliet McMaster, my sister, and Stanley Myers, whom I had married and divorced, were my two great encouragers. On an old manuscript I can still see Stanley's pale pencilled question mark by something he didn't agree with, or a pale "Cut" by a paragraph he felt was unkind. "You don't want to slaughter anyone, do you? What's the point?" Quite a contrast from Lindsay's "Don't you want revenge? Come on, now, make gleeful malice your mantra." And "gleeful malice" would be written in huge red capitals!

In November of 1993 Stanley died of cancer. Ten months later Lindsay died of a heart attack. I put the book away.

It was Lindsay's nephew who insisted on my showing a couple of chapters to a writer friend of his, hoping it would encourage me to continue. "A journalist does this better than you," said this new authority. "None of it means anything if we don't know who or what you are."

"Who or what I am?" Heavens! I did not feel encouraged, and put the book away again, this time for the junk room, where it would have stayed, but for a surprise visit from Stanley's old friend from his Balliol days, the film director Paul Almond.

"Give it to me," he said. "I'll check it out and call you from LA."

Paul is such an immediate person. He told me that when he goes to the doctor in America with some complaint, he says, "Fix it!" and they do! He called from the plane. "I've never done this before," he said. "But all I would say is – You have got to finish this book."

"You mean, 'Fix it!'" I said, laughing.

"Yes," he said. "FIX IT AND FINISH IT."

As it happened, around this time I was doing some research for my sister Julie, who was preparing a book on our great-grandfather James Clarke Hook, the Victorian seascape painter. She wanted some information about his father, James Hook, who had worked for the Foreign Office in Sierra Leone from 1842 to his death in 1850. He was required by the British Government to be Judge Arbitrator at the trials heard against Spanish and South American ships captured while slave-trading in the area. This had involved him in copious correspondence with the Foreign Office, all hand-written, to the Minister, Lord Palmerston, and signed, "I am, my lord, your lordship's most humble and obedient servant, James Hook." Now, one hundred and seventy years later at the National Archives in Kew, these letters of his were suddenly coming up on a computer screen in front of my eyes. Hundreds of them. In one he asks for a raise in his salary (£318 per year), because he'd had to replace the senior judge. His raise is refused, and one can read scrawled across the letter,

"Is there any necessity to fill this position at all? And who and what is this applicant?" It is initialled "P."

After all those endless reports and letters, so devotedly meticulous, and all written from the country called "the white man's grave" (as indeed it turned out to be), "Who and what is this applicant?"! The icy cold callousness of it made me shudder. I pressed a button and the whole thing disappeared from the screen. But I felt a brute. It was as if I had brought someone back to life, only to kill him off again.

Well, that did it.

I resolved there and then that I would go back to my book and do whatever I could to bring back to life the many characters I have worked with who, one way and another, have meant so much – and not only to me.

1

"HOME" WITH MY ELEPHANT

Recently I went to see the film *La Danse*, a French documentary about the Paris Opera Ballet housed at the Palais Garnier. I recognized at once the rehearsal room, with its round windows at the top of that beautiful theatre, because I had worked there myself during my time on Elijah Moshinsky's production of *Peter Grimes*. The dances I had created for Act III had to appear to be folk dances that the villagers knew backwards. This takes rehearsal.

I remember our surprise when the Stage Director ran up the stairs to tell us that both the Director and the Interpreter had gone home so we could stop work. *What?!* Sorry, Monsieur. It doesn't matter to us who's there, or who's not there. We work because we ourselves want to get things right. Or at least as right as they possibly can be, even if we never quite achieve what we'd hoped for. It is part of the dancer's discipline to keep on striving towards this vision of what is better and better …

Actually my father was a very disciplined person. He was no dancer, but he did love a good show as long as its intentions were honourable and had nothing to do with showing off. Showing off was a sin much frowned on in our family.

When George V died, on January 20th 1936, we were living in Kisumu, Kenya, on the shores of Lake Victoria (now Nyanza), where Daddy was Provincial Commissioner. At sundown that day – and there are the most beautiful sunsets in that baking hot part of the world – we solemnly followed Mummy out into the garden, dressed in hats and gloves. We stood with our English governess and African servant in a small circle around the flag. I was six, my sister Anthea was nine, and our brother Stephen was three. Daddy was dressed in full tropical regalia: white topee, white suit with gold braid, purple ribbon and decorations. He read some verses from the Bible, and then nodded to the *askari* (African soldier) to play the Last Post. To that mournful bugle sound the flag was slowly lowered to half mast. Daddy stood to attention, silently saluting, while Mummy wept. There was no audience, just the certain knowledge that the same loyal ceremonies were going on, hundreds of them, all over the British Empire, a return for the trust Britain had placed in her colonial servants.

Daddy was pro-African, and as a result had to endure the slings and arrows of the White Settler. His refusal to buy land (deeming it to belong to the Africans) made him unpopular. He fought hard against female circumcision, but felt that the Mission education of the day, and indeed any forcing of the pace towards the adaptation to British ideas, to be "unnatural." Mummy didn't share his concern for African welfare. She loved her birds, her animals, and her children running about barefoot. She missed England dreadfully, and was enormously proud of her family – the artistic, nature-loving and inventive Hooks. After every three-year "tour" Daddy would be given six months' "home leave," and Mummy would usually manage to stretch her stay by two or three months. To the colonials, "Home" was England (to us home was Africa). The colonials were labeled "more British than the British," and that may have been true, because I can remember, when I finally came to live in England, how astounded I was that no one had heard of Empire Day, and hardly any of St. George's Day. To us both days were great occasions.

The Empire Day parade would begin around 10 a.m., and Daddy, having organized most of it, would stand by the flagstaff to take the salute. There were Girl Guides and Boy Scouts of every race, Kavirondo chiefs with ostrich feathers and ivory teeth neckbands, the King's African Rifles, and every sort of contingent, from the British Legion to the local Mission band. Later, there would be a fête in the park, or perhaps in our garden, to which every-one came; and always a dinner party at the end of the day, with the toast "The King!" and "Three Cheers for His Majesty!" For St. George's Day, Mummy's green dragon dinner service would come out from the pantry we called the Snake Room (two puff adders had been found living there when we first arrived, and later a mamba – which was battered to death by the kitchen *toto*, a mere boy of a servant). For dinner there'd be roast beef, cape gooseberry pie, and roses in the finger bowls. All this at a temperature of 90 degrees plus. Too hot to sleep, Anthea and I would usually sit up under our mosquito nets in the nursery and listen to it all, sometimes creep out to pinch something off the servants as they dashed back and forth from the dining room to the outside kitchen. Here Juma, our Swahili cook, sweated over the wood-fire stove. His three wives lived with him in the appalling servants' quarters at the back of the house, and his children played in the open drains with the chickens and muscovy ducks, which, when they weren't copulating, added to the general grime. We were all used to the mixture of pomp and squalor, and took it as a matter of course. Even Juma, when he went for a walk, expected his three wives to follow him ceremoniously, in order of seniority.

Our education may not have been the greatest, but it suited us fine. Our governess taught us to read, write, and do sums. Mummy taught us French from a book that began "*Madame Souris a une maison*"; and we taught ourselves to draw and paint. In the afternoons Mummy would read us Dickens and Robert Louis Stevenson, and on the days she was busy we'd play for hours with our dolls. Quite often my sister Anthea would make up a play with them, usually a detective story, where we had to guess who the murderer was. As it was invariably Richard the orange monkey or Harold the long-legged brown monkey, that wasn't very difficult, but we loved it just the same.

Fiz aged five dancing at home in Ngong, Kenya 1935.

I think it must have been clear to everyone that I could dance. Mummy never praised me – that wasn't her way – but she encouraged me by always finding me a teacher wherever we were. In Kisumu it was the bank manager's wife of the Standard Bank of India. In her sitting-room above the bank she taught me the hornpipe and the Irish jig. Often on a dinner party night I'd hear Daddy's footsteps clomp-clomping down the stone passages. I'd pretend to be asleep under my mosquito net, knowing that he'd come to fetch me to dance for the guests. It didn't make any difference.

"Eleanor."

"Yes, Daddy." I wouldn't have dared to disobey him. He'd haul me off to hop and skip in my pyjamas while he whistled his favourite Gilbert and Sullivan tunes

But Anthea and I did have a secret of our own. Riding around on our bikes, we had been well aware of an Indian cinema being built opposite the Londiani Stores. One morning when we heard the music blaring out we stopped and called on the Ismaili manager to ask if we could go in and watch the film. He was horrified: Europeans, Asians and Africans did *not* mix in public places. Unperturbed, Anthea reminded him that His Highness the Aga Khan had stayed in our house (even he was not allowed in a European hotel); and she could show him a photograph of His Highness with his arm around her shoulders. It did the trick. Touched by Divinity, we got an instant free pass, and on the mornings the manager ran his films before the scheduled run, he allowed the pair of us to sit there in solitary splendour, not understanding a single word, but totally entranced by dashing young men falling from the branches of a tree onto the back of a passing horse, galloping off against the sun; dancing princesses ogling some dark-haired beefy man in jodhpurs half hidden in an archway.... We'd happily lap up yards of Indian romance before biking home to beat the mid-day sun.

The War put an end to our colonial lives. Things changed, not overnight, but pretty quickly. I remember the farewell ceremonies for Daddy, garlands of frangipani placed around his neck and long speeches about his just and fair administration. He was to be Liaison Officer for East Africa, which meant he was to travel to wherever there were East African troops: Abyssinia, North Africa, India, and later Burma and the Far East. Our governess joined up, and Mummy bought a place in the Highlands above Nairobi, near to the Limuru Girls' School.

So by September 1940 we girls, by now four of us with Valentine and Juliet, went to school for the first time. I was eleven. Our poor brother Stephen was sent to boarding school aged eight, in the old tradition. I think Mummy wanted to recreate for us something of the life she had had as one of eleven children at Silverbeck, the Hook family home in Surrey. She bought us lots of animals – a donkey, a pig, masses of rabbits, guinea pigs, hamsters and mice, several cats, a parrot, and two dogs. There was a waterfall in the grounds, a beautiful valley garden, and a view that overlooked the Ngong Hills and, on a clear day, Mount Kilimanjaro. I think it meant a lot to Mummy to have a place of her own; to be able, with her generous spirit, to be a Lady Bountiful. She filled the house with officers on leave or convalescing. She gave them a "home from home," and her Visitors' Book bears witness to their huge appreciation.

Some talk of the joys of Durban,
And some of "Snookey" too,
Of Cairo and Nairobi
And places such as these.
But in none of the spots I've stayed in
(I think you'll all agree)
Have I met with greater kindness
Than at the "Fazanerie."

We children became rather brattish. On the days when I felt the urge to get away, I'd sit with our ayah Hadija in her concrete quarters, and – aged about twelve or thirteen – smoke Gold Flake cigarettes with her, while she acted out wonderful memories of tribal warfare which her grandfather had handed down to her. She'd climb on the old beer crate she used as a table and look out of the window as though watching for the Masai. Once alerted she'd creep, bent double, round the stone floor, pushing her way through imaginary undergrowth, and stopping dead still from time to time to pick up a scent or a sound.

Whenever I could I'd go with her to an *ngoma* (an African shindig). Occasionally Mummy would give permission for this to happen on our land. The dancers, among them our *mpishi* (cook) and his wife, would stamp out a circle and surround it with a fence of wattle sticks. At nightfall, as if by magic, the Kikuyu would appear from miles around. An open fire burned in the centre of the circle; a few hurricane lamps hung on the fence, and drummers beat out a rhythm that whipped up some wild and abandoned dancing. I'd crouch against the fence in the dark, the only white face there, always a little afraid; perhaps even a bit possessed, for it was around this time that my sisters would tease me about my habit of what they called "gazing into space" – i.e. pretending to listen while off on some flight of imagination, or more probably trying to work something out in my head. Today, horrible thought, I might be given pills for Attention Deficit Disorder.

A chorus line as I first saw one. Kenya 1930s.

By 1944 it became clear to us that our parents had split up. Mummy had fallen for an army major who, with the years, turned out to be a kind and caring stepfather. But we weren't to know that; and when you have no experience to relate to, the fear of abandonment looms large. I remember at the time my sister Juliet found me crying alone on the verandah. When she asked me what the matter was, I told her she was too young to understand; but that she wouldn't be my baby sister any more. At six years of age she couldn't work out what could possibly happen to stop her being my baby sister. She still can't − nor can I ! Maybe I thought that one break-up must inevitably lead to another. I don't know. But there isn't a child in the world who escapes the pain of their parents' divorce. You put it out of your mind and find a way − bury yourself in books perhaps, football or computers. My own way was to go to a back room, wind up the gramophone, and dance for hours on end, imagining myself to be Ginger Rogers, Jessie Matthews, or Eleanor Powell.

One day, some family friends − Esther and Cyril Garnham, a couple who hadn't seen their children in England since the start of the War − told my mother that if they ever found an escape route to England, they'd take me with them, so that I might be properly trained as a dancer. Dr Garnham, a malaria specialist, was also an excellent musician. I would sometimes dance about while he was practising the piano. I owe him a great deal in that he persuaded my parents that training was important and it should not be denied me.

Amazingly, the Garnhams found their escape route. My mother wrote to Ninette de Valois and to my godmother in Wimbledon. Daddy said he was pleased I had chosen something I wanted to do. I shut up. It seemed more like Fate to me. But never mind; for in March 1945, as a very raw fifteen-year-old with my toy elephant in his new warm clothes, I waved goodbye to my beloved home and family, and set off down the Nile to board a troopship at Alexandria. After a rather luxurious journey through Juba, Khartoum, Luxor and Cairo, my adopted family and I finally walked up the gangway of our ship. As we stepped on board, we were each handed a tin mug. I looked at mine, and I remember very clearly saying to myself, "I think your life has changed."

As there were still German U-boats about, we travelled in convoy: three big troop ships with two to four thousand persons on board, surrounded by eight destroyers. Our boat was the *Alcantara*, with two thousand passengers. I shared a cabin with eight missionaries who looked 102 to me, with their hair in low buns, their long tweed skirts and knickers down to their knees. No doubt with the best intentions, they made me read the emergency drill that was pinned to the back of the cabin door. I nearly fainted. Our lifeboat was 12A – the one between 12 and 14. It didn't fool me for an instant. But we survived, and on May 23rd, 1945, we anchored in Glasgow, where I found I couldn't understand a word the dockers were saying. I was a foreigner. Yet this was the place I'd always heard referred to as "Home."

Standing on the deck with my stuffed elephant, the little passport I had made for him ready in my pocket, we stared down at this new home. It looked cold and rather drab, but it was land, and we liked it at once. A few days later I found myself actually standing at the barre in the ballet room at Sadlers Wells Theatre. I was a little brown-skinned savage compared to the pale sophisticated dancers who surrounded me. Petrified, and not knowing what to expect, or what was expected of me, I was held together by an awareness that this was what I'd always wanted to do. This was what my parents had so willingly allowed me to do. No more dreaming of Home; this was it.

"First positions, everyone, please."

I kept my eyes glued to the girl in front of me to copy her every move.

"Here we go then! Ready ... AND ..."

With that first *plié* I started my own life.

2

THE FORCES OF DESTINY

My godmother had kindly agreed to put me up – not that easy in those days of rationing and clothing coupons. Our family friends, the Garnhams, left me at her house, and not without a qualm. There was something grim about the door bell – a handle at the end of a long chain. When you pulled it you could faintly hear a bell clanging somewhere at the back. A maid with a club foot came to the door and explained that everyone was out, so we went outside to walk in the garden. Not a single flower anywhere – just rows of "Dig for Victory" vegetables, some gooseberry bushes, and an air raid shelter. Down by the greenhouses there was a bee-hive. The bees sounded like hornets to me.

This was Wimbledon. This was where my god-mother still lived in fast-fading suburban grandeur. Her stock-broker husband (to whom she seldom spoke) now occupied the rooms behind the garage where the chauffeur once lived. Two of their children were in the forces, another at Cambridge, and their daughter at boarding school. This meant I was alone with the two parents, who were kind and civil to me but not to each other.

Eager to please and not seem a burden or spoiled colonial brat, I endeavoured to be a model of good behaviour, and would divide my time between the two of them: one evening in the drawing-room with her, talking about queues and rationing, and the next in the library with him, listening to bomb stories, which he hoped would make me laugh.

Daytime I spent at Sadlers Wells, to which they turned a somewhat disapproving eye. I felt it, but it didn't affect me because I was so conscious of my own good fortune in being there, and being classically trained by teachers such as Vera Volkova, Ailne Phillips and Peggy van Praagh, with Ninette de Valois herself checking on our progress. It's still a mystery to me why I was accepted at all. My mother was not a theatre person. She had written to Ninette de Valois enclosing a photo of me standing on the lawn at our home in Limuru, Kenya, because de Valois was the only person from the ballet world she'd heard of. Perhaps Mummy included one or two good reports, but I doubt that would have made any difference. My guess is that Madam de Valois worked out that anyone aged fifteen – travelling thousands of miles in wartime to be trained as a dancer – just maybe had something. It may have helped that there were some talented South Africans in her company. But I'll never know the exact reason, for in those happy days before apprehension sets in I just accepted that I'd been accepted, and concentrated only on the work I had to do to be any sort of a dancer.

Every morning I would catch the 93 bus to South Wimbledon and then take the underground to the Angel Islington. It was a little frightening as the underground train windows were taped criss-cross against bomb blast, leaving just a small hole in the centre through which if you were lucky you could catch the name of the station.

I soon learned, to my horror, that men *do* make passes at girls who wear glasses. And to avoid these very frightening advances, I decided the best way would be to make ugly faces the whole journey, so that no one would want to come near me. There are a lot of stations from South Wimbledon to the Angel Islington and I'd arrive with my poor face aching from the strain. I wouldn't have dared tell my godmother about these groping men. She would think it my fault.

I don't remember feeling particularly lonely. But I do remember feeling very different – almost a foreigner – because I was born in Africa.

This rather precarious existence couldn't last; and nor did it. It was shattered one morning at breakfast. The Allies were opening up the concentration camps, and the horrific photographs and reports were all over the newspapers for the first time. It is bad enough to read of the Holocaust today; but when it was first discovered it was absolutely terrifying. Human atrocity beyond the wildest imagination. I shoved the papers away from me and stood up. My godmother and her husband seemed preoccupied. Was this something they expected of the enemy? I didn't know – in any case they were silent. I went upstairs to my room and sat on my bed, hand on elephant, and stared at the cupboard. I was convinced this was a nightmare place that I had come to, and I just wanted to get out. I grabbed my practice clothes and ran for the 93 bus.

An opportunity to escape arose that evening – well … almost.

Just as we were finishing dinner, Ada the maid came in to tell me there was a friend of mine in the hall. A friend? Who did I know?

I ran out, and there was Alison, a girl I had met on board ship some weeks previously.

"Alison! What are you doing here?" I was very pleased to see her.

"I've run away."

"*What*?!"

"I've run away to you. I don't know anyone else."

"But you can't stay here." My mind raced. They'll never accept this. All that rationing – I'm bad enough. And worse, Alison was rather a flighty girl who had chased the sailors on the ship. These puritan Scots will die.

"Wait!" I said. And I went back in to make up some story about Alison missing her train, and could she stay the night? Oh, no thanks, she didn't need to use the telephone – she had arranged to meet her father the next day. Whether I was believed or not I have no idea. Alison and I went upstairs and whispered for hours.

It turned out that her grandmother, whom she'd been longing to meet, lived in a squalid flat above her shop, and was very bad-tempered. For Alison, used to servants and space, this was a bit of a shock.

"I'm not going back," she said. "You're lucky."

"Well..."

"*And* I don't like the people here."

"No. Quite." Pause for much thought. And plans for the next day.

"And you still say 'Quite'!" she said, as we drowsed off.

The next morning we were up bright and early, having planned that Alison should come with me to Sadlers Wells, after which I could telephone my aunts at Bexhill-on-Sea, who I was sure would know what to do. Auntie Bea was a Girl Guide.

Looking over the banisters as we went downstairs, we saw that the hall was full of police! We were told that Alison's father was in the study with my godmother.

It was all over – her bid for freedom, and my credibility.

I don't think we spoke, but at the gate Alison turned round and we exchanged looks as two hostages might, surrounded by terrorists in an unfamiliar land. I never saw or heard from Alison again, but in that look we exchanged I recognized the rebel in myself.

My godmother on reflection decided I should go to boarding school. She chose the Cone-Ripman School at Tring in Hertfordshire. My father telephoned me from Nairobi – a personal call, but before he was put through I was warned that the Japanese would be listening to the call.

"Is this what you want??" Daddy asked. "I thought you were so happy at Sadlers Wells."

"I know, Daddy," I replied, with my godmother standing firmly beside me, and the Japs decoding every word. "But it's all right, Daddy. It *is* a dancing school."

It was run by two wonderful Jewish women: Miss Gracie Cone (with the help of her sisters Miss Lillie and Miss Valerie) and Mrs Ripman. Both had been excellent dancers in their day.

They had bought the Rothschilds' mansion at Tring, which they probably got for a song. No one wanted the large stately home in 1945. The country was enormously in debt after the War, Churchill had been ousted, and it was the start of the new Socialist era under Atlee. My mother's cousin Clare Rich had handed over her own stately home to the American army during the War. I read a touching letter from her saying, "I've just been offered £15 for Daddy's Rolls, but I can't bear to let it go under £25."

The Rothschild family would have been relieved to know that their grand mansion had been taken over by a ballet school. The large reception rooms made excellent dance studios, and the many bedrooms, turned into dormitories, could house us all. We slept on Land Army bunks; in fact I think the whole place was furnished by army surplus stuff. No rugs anywhere on those wooden floors, and in the winter we were bitterly cold. We ate in the basement, in what would have been the pantries and sculleries of the old house. We took it in turns to help the old man-servant wash up. The cloths were always soaking wet, and the sight of the piles of scraps in an old pail would send me rushing into the corridor to hide my "sick noises." It was important to us all to appear "wartime friendly."

The staff was mixed, some excellent, some dotty, some refugees. We worked long hours, studying every type of dance as well as drama, music, musical appreciation, and ballet history. September 1945 was its very first term; and in September 1946 I was the first girl to be awarded their "Shield of Merit."

While we were there, Mavis Traill and I choreographed a ballet. She was the Ugly Duckling that turned into a beautiful Swan, and I was the mother Duck with a mass of ducklings. Amazingly this amateur work won the Pavlova Casket at the Sunshine Ballet competitions in London. And Traill recently reminded me that at some end-of-term do I had choreographed a comedy tap routine. I was the front legs of a horse and my friend Maggie Price was the back legs. Braving the boards to a 40s pop song, we clopped our way through a dotty softshoe shuffle. Traill says it was very funny. Perhaps I was showing signs of becoming a choreographer and a clown.

I was at Tring for two years; and I did a further year at the School's London Studio, during which time we were encouraged to do outside classes and audition for jobs. The school was well run and eventually became known as the Arts Educational. The standard was high, and I met and was inspired by many wonderful dancers there, some of whom are my friends to this day: Mavis Traill, Sheila O'Neil, Diana Monks, Antoinette Sibley, Aleta Morrison, and the late Daphne Dale, John Gilpin and Leslie Crowther.

Traill and I shared a room in Tedworth Square, Chelsea. It cost three guineas a week – thirty-one shillings and sixpence each. In London the old family houses that had managed to escape the bombing were now turned into rooming houses and bed-sits, occupied to a large extent by men who had been demobbed from the forces and were now looking for work. Our room had two beds, a cupboard, and a gas metre for the gas fire and a gas ring on which we could boil a kettle or cook something. Each house would have one bathroom, but rather than queue up for it, we mostly used the basin in the corner of the room in which to wash ourselves and our clothes.

We called each other by our surnames. Even after much water under the bridge – husbands, children, births and deaths, Traill is still Traill to me, as I am Fazan to her.

It felt very good to have a place of our own. We were both rather scared of our Irish landlady, and Traill was particularly horrified by her slightly mad daughter. The whole place was rather odd, but perhaps typical of the times. In the basement there was a prostitute, we students on the ground floor, above us Frank, a demobbed lieutenant who had found a job being shot out of a cannon at the circus, and on the top floor an often drunken weirdo lot from the Chelsea upper-class set. Sometimes at night we'd hear them crashing and falling about on the stairs, and it would terrify me. I'd heave the suitcases down from the top of the cupboard and say, "Traill, we're leaving!" Where to, heaven only knows. And Traill, more down-to-earth than I, would look up from her book and say, "Put them away, Fazan!"

We tried to teach Frank how to bow when he landed – shot from a cannon onto the net! He said it wasn't worth it, because he'd lost all dignity crawling and falling about in the net before he could get to the platform. However, we made him raise his arms, and (in our cramped space) turn slowly round, as though facing an enormous audience and thunderous applause. Poor Frank, he wasn't very good at it, and one night he knocked on our door to tell us he'd been given the sack. His claustrophobia had got the better of him, and he'd shouted from the depths of the cannon, "Let me out! Let me out of here!" Frank had clearly been knocking back the booze with the clowns, for he was sick in our basin. The next day he slipped a note of apology under our door which ended, "I shall never darken your door again." And for some reason we found this highly amusing.

Well, we were students – ballet students – and we walked with our feet turned out and hair pinned back. That was our statement – there was no "youth culture." My godmother's husband came to visit us one evening, and we gave him supper – herrings, I seem to remember. He was appalled by our little room, or pretended to be; and, to our great amusement, kept repeating, "Now I know why girls go wrong."

I was happy at the Cone-Ripman School: *really* happy to be learning so much without feeling I was a burden to anyone. The fact that my poor father was forking out for all of this didn't seem to bother me, although as soon as I got my second job I wrote to tell him he no longer needed to send me an allowance.

He wrote back, sending me £100 and quoting, "To thine own self be true; And it must follow, as the night the day, Thou can'st not then be false to any man..." I was touched, but I had no idea who mine own self might be....

3

THE CHANCE OF A LIFETIME: GEORGE ROBEY

Oh happy little circus girl
  So proud and gay
  Come take your place in pleasure's whirl
  And dance away;
  Laugh on while sunshine still endures
  And laugh you may;
  A short and merry life is yours
  A life of brief today.

So sang Ethel Hayden in *The Circus Girl* in 1896. Half a century later I was laughing and dancing with her husband in *The Windmill Man*. It was pleasure's whirl all right. He was George Robey – known as "The Prime Minister of Mirth."

(Hulton archive/getty images)

George Robey with his wife Blanche Littler backstage 1944.

George Robey had started his career in the Music Hall in 1891 at the age of twenty-two. He'd soon become one of England's most popular comedians, playing equally successfully in revue, pantomime, farce, and musicals. Laurence Olivier cast George Robey as the dying Falstaff in his film of *Henry V.* During the 1914-18 war, Robey's fame was such that he was used to recruit soldiers; it won him the CBE. He also produced: in 1907 he gave George Formby Senior his first big chance. I'm proud to add that in the spring of 1948, it was George Robey who gave me my first job: a dancer in a chorus line of twelve. Our show, *The Windmill Man,* belonged to the world of simple pleasures. Apart from the seventy-nine-year-old George Robey as the Windmill Man, the cast included his old friend Bransby Williams, aged seventy-eight and famous for his Dickensian monologues; the Colleano Brothers – a low comedy act with two brothers, a wife and a nephew; eight singers; twelve dancers, and a trick cyclist from Belgium called Charlie Kaye. We didn't see much of the acts ourselves, as we were too busy running up and down stairs changing for the next number. We were, however, able to glimpse something of them at the Monday band calls; and I do remember being fearfully impressed by Bransby Williams at the dress rehearsal, doing his Bill Sikes from *Oliver Twist*. It was quite gruesome, dimly lit and very dramatic. A front-cloth scene, as all his turns were. And we enjoyed the Colleano Brothers dressed as two ancient ballerinas doing a dance to "The Flight of the Bumble Bee," with an enormous balloon sandwiched between them. It exploded on the final note.

Sundays were spent travelling and checking into our theatrical digs. We never knew quite what to expect. One of the singers told me that when he'd opened the door of his allocated bedroom a voice from within croaked out, "Is it night or day?" He closed the door and fled!

We were booked to tour Glasgow, Blackpool, Lewisham and Brighton. If the show was a success we might go on.

By now George Robey was married to Blanche Littler, the producer of our show. She was a rather dignified woman who always wore a hat and carried her purse tucked under her arm as older people seemed to. She was actually thirty years younger than her husband and part of a well known theatrical family. Her parents had managed the Woolwich theatre and her two younger brothers, Emile and Prince Littler, had worked their way up to becoming powerful West End producers. Prince Littler was the manager of Drury Lane and the Coliseum, among other theatres, and also managed the Stoll Theatre group with its theatres all over the country. Before the war it was normal practice to have a touring version of a successful London show–sometimes two or three, known as Number One, Two, and Three tours, depending on the size of the theatre and the importance of the provincial town. These tours would publicise the show and nurture talent for future productions. I doubt the Littlers actually owned the bricks and mortar of any of the theatres they managed. It didn't matter. They were hands-on producers, working quite outside any class structures, as theatre people mostly do. Typically their mother, Mrs Littler, toured with our show, working as George Robey's dresser. It was a family show in every sense, and nepotism a natural part of it. Blanche Littler may have seen the *The Windmill Man* as a vehicle for her husband, believing his appeal to be as great as it once had been, or possibly–with *Soldiers in Skirts*, a romp for the Forces, still touring the provinces – there would be room for a family show; but in reality the days of simple pleasures had already passed. Not that we were aware of this; we were "professionals" on six pounds a week, and we would dance as happily for an audience of twenty as we did for one of fifty. There were seldom more.

Every night before the performance, George Robey would tout for the show. He would stand outside the theatre in full make-up and costume, handing out sketched portraits of himself to anyone passing. Each one had been drawn and signed by him on the inside of an old cigarette packet, and he had hundreds. His mother-in-law Mrs Littler stood behind him ready with spares. These she stored in her enormous knitting bag which she was never without– handy should anyone want one. Sometimes we'd lean out of the windows at the top of the theatre where we dressed to watch him shuffling up and down the street in his bowler hat and clown make-up, chatting up anyone who'd stop. Few did. The passing crowds mostly hurried past. It never seemed odd, or touching – stars did that sort of thing, we thought.

Train calls were best, for this was a time when we'd all get together. A couple of carriages would be reserved for us with *The Windmill Man* pasted on the outside. I'd save George Robey a seat with a table, as we both liked to draw. I'd wait to see him shuffle down the platform on the arm of his mother-in-law and wave to him from the window. One day he drew a caricature of himself for me. I still have it. At the time I had no idea that he had exhibited his watercolours at the Royal Academy, nor that he was a superb violin maker. He'd greet us at the door of the carriage with his tummy stuck out, saying: "Punch it, girls! Go on – punch it." We rather dreaded this game. Traill always said she gave it the most feeble of punches in case she did him in, but I, not liking it much either, would give him a really hefty punch and stagger back in giggling defeat. He loved this. His stomach was as tough and hard as any athlete's, and he was proud of that. At lunch time we'd unwrap our sandwiches and he would make me laugh by pulling faces and waggling his eyebrows at the fillings; rationing was still at its height. We must have made strange companions. He was almost eighty and I was just eighteen.

My first shake up came all too soon. There are rules that must be adhered to even, or perhaps particularly, in family shows. One of the girls got the sack. She'd spent the night with Lynne Colleano. That was a shock in itself, but now she hadn't turned up for the opening number. We managed to get through that without her, dash up the flights of stairs, change, and rush back on for the Military Tap – a precision dance in which we were all dressed as identical skittles. Half way through, peering through the holes in our masks, we could just make out the missing skittle as she tottered unsteadily on. She was drunk, with her mask back to front and lipstick smirched all over her face, quite unable to find her place – bumping and crashing into each skittle in turn. The audience clapped and hooted, those that were there, and one by one each skittle shook with the giggles. All, that is, except me. Squinting through the holes in my mask (I'm very short sighted), this lurching colleague struck me as an appalling vision of life gone wrong. I nearly fainted.

As we changed frantically for the Flower Ballet, Traill helped me off with my mask. "What on earth's the matter with you, Fazan? You look awful. Hey, shut up everyone, Fazan is about to be sick. Someone else better dance the Rose Queen." What? The Rose Queen was the principal role in the Flower Ballet. No one was going to dance

that role but me! Just as they say in showbiz stories...
I recovered.

The final scene – the George Robey spot – was a trial
scene and we were a jury of dolls. We sat there oo-ing and
ah-ing and batting our eyelids, not really understanding
that George Robey had brilliantly reversed the popular
Music Hall trend for the down-and-out who masquerades
as a toff, to the Toff who (through booze) had become a
down-and-out. Two singers dressed as policemen shoved
George Robey into the dock. In his bowler hat and clergy-
man's coat, he shook them off with: "I have not come here
to be made a laughing stock of. Please remember where
you are." Then he'd rattle off at tremendous speed: "One
finds on statistical evidence that the authentic revelations
are diabolically inconsistent with the idiosyncrasies of our
qualifications, or, in other words, the allegorical excavations
of a bygone contraption are, or should be, dictographically
corroborated by the quintessence of conciseness and if I
can't spell all that, I can say it." (Music cue.)

I like to go walking along by myself
It's merely for exercise
I wander along like a mischievous elf
But I always expect a surprise.
T'other day I was walking longside of a hedge
The hedge was apropos of some trees
I got my surprise as I walked 'long the edge
'Twas a sound wafted my way on the breeze.
So I stopped, and I looked, and I listened.
First I thought it was here
Then I thought it was there

A peculiar sound I really declare
I've heard it before but I cannot say where –
So I stopped, and I looked, and I listened,
Someone said "YOU... ," someone said "Don't..."
Someone said "Do... ," someone said "Won't..."
So I stopped... and I looked... and I left.

And so he did, waving his hat as the curtain fell. The calls followed quickly, his being the last; eyebrows raised, he'd give that cherubic smile left and right and raise his hat to the gods. There wasn't much applause, but then there weren't many there. *Annie Get Your Gun* had just opened at the Coliseum, and *Oklahoma* was filling the house at Drury Lane. There was no competing. George Robey relied, as he must always have done, on giving himself.

"If You Were the Only Girl in the World" was first sung by George Robey and his co-star Violet Lorraine in *The Bing Boys Are Here*– a 1916 revue that went to Broadway. "Oh How Rude" and "Bang Went the Chance of a Lifetime" were two of his famous Music Hall songs. I wish now that I had asked him to sing them, or to tell me about Dan Leno and Little Tich, whom he knew so well – but I didn't. He stuck to those old-world principles: Never swank, grouse, spill the beans, or quit.

Six years later, in 1954, Sir George Robey was knighted; he died in the same year.

It was on our final train journey from Lewisham to Brighton that the awesome seventy-nine-year-old Bransby Williams asked if I would sit with him. I didn't dare refuse.

Bransby Williams as Bill Sikes.

"I've been watching you," he said.
"Oh?"

"Tell me what a nice girl like you is doing in a profession like this?"

"Well, I do love dancing; and I hope..."

"Don't," he said. "I want you to take a good look at me now, and learn something from it. Go on, girl. Look at me."

He had very large eyes and long white hair down to his shoulders. (He looked a bit like Alistair Sim.) I stared dutifully into his face.

"You are looking at a broken old man, once a famous actor, and now touring in this tacky, third-rate show, just to get a bob or two to live on. I want you to remember what you see, and save yourself before it's too late."

4

GETTING THE LAUGHS: JACK HULBERT AND CICELY COURTNEIDGE

At Christmas 1948 Val Parnell, the impresario and son of a well-known ventriloquist, produced the first lavish production of a pantomime after the war years. It was *Cinderella*, and the programme bears witness to the times with an advertisement: "Gents' suits for hire (no coupons required)."

Evelyn Laye was the stunning and glamorous Prince Charming, with Roma Beaumont as Cinderella. Tommy Trinder was Buttons, the Bernard Brothers from America were the Ugly Sisters, and Franklin Bennet was Dame. We were a chorus of fifty dancers – yes, fifty – on £7 a week for a twice-daily show.

During the run six of us got together to form our own dance act. Should we fail to get into a ballet company when the show closed, this would be our way of getting out of the chorus.

We had only the mornings to rehearse our act, and the late nights after the show to churn away at our sewing machines making our costumes. We must have managed to impress the ballet mistress, as off her own bat she arranged for us to audition for the producer Alfred Black, who was preparing a new Variety show for the Moss Empires circuit.

We put all we had into our audition; "Slaughter on Tenth Avenue" was our hit turn and even the costumes held up. Between the shows later that night we waited on tenterhooks for the ballet mistress to give us the verdict.

"Alfred Black liked you very much, girls, but he's not sure yet what form his show will be taking. He'll let you know." It sounded simply wonderful; the carefully couched terms of brush-off were as yet unfamiliar.

"Oh, and Eleanor," she went on, "Jack Hulbert was in the stalls with Mr Black, and he'd like you to audition for his new show on Monday."

I couldn't believe it... Jack Hulbert! I'd seen him at the cinema in Nairobi with his wife Cicely Courtneidge in *Under Your Hat*; they were film stars and favourites in the West End theatre, and now Jack Hulbert had actually noticed me. I suddenly remembered the others and looked round....

"It's that grin of yours that's done it," Traill said, and everyone laughed.

That Saturday, April 2nd, 1949, I wrote in my diary: "The lights go up in Piccadilly." It was the first time since the war, and Zoe Gail, the Dandini of our pantomime, stood on the balcony of Swan and Edgar's and sang, "I'm going to get lit up when the lights go on in London." On the Sunday I've written: "Worry all day about tomorrow," and on the Monday of the audition: "Am handed a contract–Surprise." And so it was.

I was standing in the wings, dressed in my tights with my tap and pointe shoes ready, waiting, and waiting, to be called on stage to do my bit. Suddenly the long-chinned man himself – Jack Hulbert – strolled into the wings beside me, and sitting casually on the stage manager's stool, said, with his nasal elegant drawl, "Hullo, who are you?" I told him. He then asked where I lived... where my parents were... but he never mentioned work, nor that he'd seen me dance.

"In Africa, eh? And you came here on your own! By elephant, eh what?"

(Smile) "No, but I did ride a camel in Cairo."

"Hmm. Nasty brutes, camels, don't you think?"

"Yes." (Smile) "Mine tried to bite my leg."

"Did he, now? That was rather unfriendly, or was he being friendly?"

"I don't know. I didn't like it much." (Smile. His eyes narrowed.)

"Do you do anything else besides ride camels?"

"Well, actually, I'm here to audition for you as a dancer." I thought perhaps he didn't know.

"I see, you do surprise me. Perhaps then you'd better sign this." And he pulled out a contract from his pocket.

"You mean... I've got the job?" He laughed.

"Not if you're late for rehearsal. They've started over there. Chop-Chop, Africa!" I ran off, amazed and exhilarated; never mind still in the chorus – this was a West End show with an American choreographer called Bert Stimmel who had trained with Martha Graham. I joined in with gusto, but I did wonder how it was that I had got the job. Was it really just my grin?

Today I'd be aware of the games: the pecking order that has to be maintained, the compliments reserved effusively for those at the top. I might even guess that in chatting to me Jack Hulbert was checking one thing: would I respond as required to his charm?

He needn't have bothered: I fell straight away. Who hasn't fallen at one time or other for the charm of the educated English amateur? This certain charm (which has had a good innings in the British theatre) goes something like this: preferably Oxbridge, fond of long hours, secretly scornful of all endeavour, with a decided ability to manipulate others; and above all, an endearingly amateurish front. It works like a spell, and for all I know Jack may have started it all.

Son of a doctor, he was educated at Westminster and Cambridge University where he appeared in "numerous theatrical entertainments." The impresario Robert Courtneidge saw him there, and in 1913 gave Jack his first professional part as Robert Jaffray in a musical comedy called "The Pearl Girl" at the Shaftesbury. Cicely

Courtneidge played Lady Betty Viddulph. She was not only the star of the show but the boss's daughter. Jack married her, and from then on Jack and Cis were a team: only occasionally working apart, and each relying heavily on the other. Rather like Fred and Ginger, he gave her class and she gave him... well, not sex exactly... but vitality.

Vitality was Cis's stock in trade. She was a blonde, blue-eyed bombshell who sang flat out while marching up and down the stage with the odd skip, whoops and a thigh slap, to show she was not only inexhaustible but hearty and funny as well. Very funny. Her appeal to a British audience was enormous.

Our show was called *Her Excellency*, with Cis playing a British Ambassador who'd been sent out to some South American republic to obtain a beef contract. It was a topical comedy – beef was still a rarity in 1949 – and with song and dance and Jack directing, it must have seemed like a good bet.

During rehearsals it was clear that Cicely Courtneidge was very much the star of the show. She was always expensively dressed, and rather intimidating to her colleagues. Thorley Walters, who played her Attaché (in more ways than one, it was said), was the one person for whom she seemed to have great affection and admiration. He was a lovely man and a talented comedy actor; but whenever he asked any of us out, we were carefully distant in case anything got back. Meanwhile Jack was living on and off with a beautiful ex-dancer in Baker Street; but this was middle-class theatre and infidelity was hush-hush and accepted. In any case there was no doubting their alliance;

everything – every number, every scene – was arbitrarily altered by Jack until Cis was satisfied. How many hours into the night did we wave our cloaks in the bull fight number while Cis perfected her quick change from Ambassador to Matador in ten seconds flat? It was technique that counted, not talent, and poor Billy Dainty as the Bull was cursed for forgetting the changes while Bert Stimmel sat silently in the corner watching his choreography disintegrate before his eyes. It did not occur to us to question anything.

Jack, as producer, would stride up and down the stalls smacking his forehead, but he was always lovably boyish in the breaks. He'd go to the window with his hands in his pockets, look up at the sky and whistle, "Phew, that's a Spitfire, by Jove," and (with a sidelong glance to see if you were looking), "He's going at quite a lick." Or he'd stand in the middle of the floor rocking backwards and forwards on his heels, absorbed in thought, and whistling a jolly snatch. Suddenly he'd break into a few rather heavy tap steps, shake his head and do it again. Once he had everyone's attention he'd go into a rather longer tap break, finishing with a wobbly turn and "Back to work, boys and girls!" It had nothing to do with the show we were in; but I swear I would have done anything for him.

We opened in Glasgow, and rehearsals continued all day, and after the show at night. We thought it was fun because the actors gave us tea and gin in their dressing rooms, and we'd be in on their moaning. It gave us a sense of intimacy; and it helped, for we were working like slaves, and with our dressing rooms at the top of the theatre, we were often hard put to make our changes in time. I once missed an entrance by seconds....

(Knock, Knock)

"Yes, who is it?" (Growled)

"It's Eleanor, Miss Courtneidge. I've come to apologise for being late for the bull fight tonight."

"Late? Why were you late?"

"My cloak was buried under the Samba hats."

"You must check your costumes before the show, not during."

"Yes, I'm very sorry. Goodnight, Miss Courtneidge" (getting out as fast as I could).

"And cheer up," she said, as I reached the door. "Go out and have a large gin or two – what what!" She wanted to be friendly, but the success of the show – *her* show – was all-consuming. I doubt she thought of anything else.

The actors' moans soon turned to despondency. All their best lines and their laughs were taken away from them and given to Cis so that she, and she alone, might shine. Should anyone get a laugh during a performance, the others would say: "Fool! That'll be gone by tomorrow." The show got steadily worse, and only Eleanor Summerfield, who was playing the vivacious and vamping daughter of the South American beef King, managed to keep something going, and the audience loved her. In Southsea she got her cards – two weeks' notice and no explanation. I don't think she bothered to ask for one; it had been said in a newspaper that she was a younger version of Cis. No one blamed Jack.

When the show finally opened at the London Hippodrome the reviews were all much the same – meagre. One critic wrote: "A voice from the gallery called 'Good old Cis, it wasn't your fault' which was at once accurate and compassionate. Miss Courtneidge put everything she had into her work, without a tuneful song or witty line, and battling away on her own, even her vivacity cannot lift *Her Excellency* out of mediocrity." My first lesson in what the critics don't, and cannot, know.

The show ran for nine months; due very possibly to the fact that Cis, summoning all her incredible vitality, gave her "Please tell your friends to come and see us" speech at the end of every performance. This was a tradition before the theatre became snobbish.

I cried when the show closed – "Here Today and Gone Tomorrow" takes a lot of getting used to. I was really glad to read in the newspapers some time later that Jack had been awarded the CBE, and Cis had been made a Dame of the British Empire.

Twenty years later I was working as the choreographer on a Barry Humphries movie. One of the numbers was to be the cabaret of a seedy night club, where Aunt Edna (she wasn't a Dame then) was having a night out. The show was to start innocently and then turn into a strip so that Aunt Edna could get her outraged reactions. We decided on Marie Antoinette surprised in her boudoir by a revolutionary who, during a pitiful struggle, removes all her clothes. The number was well cast: Fiona Richmond of *Playboy* fame was Marie Antoinette, and a girl from the Rocky

Horror Show was the revolutionary. I had only one day to rehearse this number–a Sunday–and the girls arrived in good time. Fiona turned up in white mink and showed me her new sports car, a present from Paul Raymond (the impresario of the strip-club, Raymond's Revue Bar) with a suitably intimate number plate. Rocky Horror, who had carrot-dyed hair, came for some reason dressed as Charlie Chaplin with a bowler hat, white dickey and cane. I went with them to the caretaker to find out which room we were to work in.

"They're all booked," he said.

"What?" I couldn't believe it. "But I came here myself to book it, and it was you who assured me it was down in the book."

"You're quite right, Miss; I'll go and tell the lot on the top floor to shove off."

"Yes, please do," I said, for we were due to shoot the next day and if the number was going to be funny, it needed work. After a few minutes the caretaker called down from the top of the stairs:

"You can come up now. They're leaving."

"Thanks," I yelled back. "Come on, ladies."

As we started up the stairs we could hear the disgruntled troupe descending. Rounding the bend, to my horror I recognised amongst the displaced troupers, two familiar faces – Jack Hulbert CBE and Dame Cis.

My first thought was to run downstairs and tell the caretaker, "It's alright! They can have it! Please go up and tell them they can have it!" But the pro in me couldn't allow it. My next impulse was to greet them warmly and say, "Remember me? I was your favourite girl," but that seemed unwise. I then did something I'm really ashamed of: I put my head down and walked silently through them.

While the girls got changed, or rather threw down their paraphernalia, I looked out of the window. Jack and Cis and their group had all gathered forlornly in the street below around that sports car, wondering where to go next. In their eighties, and still at it; still chopping and changing, no doubt, and pinching the laughs for Cis. Maybe, who knows, rehearsing a replacement for someone who had been too good to last...

But just at that moment I wanted to fling open the window and shout down, like that man in the gallery: "Good old Jack! Good old Cis! It isn't your fault. It was never your fault. The English loved you. Remember? All through the War. Before and after. You were wonderful. Can you hear me? *Wonderful* ..." But I didn't do it. Instead I turned back and got on with the tricky business of working out a comedy scene that would (Hullo!) make sure that Aunt Edna would get her laughs.

5

WHERE BLUEBIRDS FLY: STANISLAS IDZIKOWSKI

The dancer Stanislas Idzikowski has been variously described by his peers as having had "phenomenal elevation," "dazzling technique," and he was a brilliant mime. I am able to vouch for the truth of this, for although I only knew him in his late fifties and as my teacher, he corrected us by his own demonstration–a privilege I'll not forget.

Idzikowski was born in Warsaw in 1894, and had studied with the great ballet master Enrico Cecchetti. He danced first with Pavlova and her company, and later with the Diaghilev company where Leonide Massine created many roles for him: the Cat in *Contes Russe*, the Dandy in *Boutique Fantastique* and Harlequin in *Carnival*. By all accounts he was a phenomenal Bluebird.

Photograph of Stanislas Idzikowski inscribed to Eleanor.

He came to England several times with the Diaghilev company, and some time in the 1920s left them to guest at the Vic Wells Ballet, creating a further role in Ashton's *Les Rendezvous* in 1933. Happily he stayed on and took up teaching. Five foot, or five foot four at the most, Idzikowski had led a hard life, and was endowed with that curious mixture one often meets in dancers–a child-like simplicity together with a worldly acceptance of the way things are. Nevertheless, great dancer that he was, one couldn't help sensing an underlying bitterness in him.

"They like you while you are a star," he said to me one day with a wry smile, and told me of the time when he had been ill with a temperature of 105 and had been carried from the hotel in Monte Carlo wrapped in a blanket, shoved on stage to dance the Bluebird, wrapped up again and carried back to bed.

"Was there no understudy for you, Maestro?" I asked. He just stared at me and I realised my mistake at once... Of course, there could be no cover for Idzikowski.

It was clear that if you wanted to remain a dancer, it was strength of character that was needed. Talent, and working at technique, were taken for granted and never anything one talked about.

Leonide Massine writes that in 1925, while choreographing the Cochrane-Coward revue *On with the Dance*, he walked up Shaftesbury Avenue to visit the 75-year-old ballet master, Enrico Cecchetti, in his studio. He found Idzikowski there, helping the old man to get his complex method of teaching down onto paper. This became the Cecchetti Technique that is taught in dance schools all over the world. Having been largely responsible for its preservation, Idzikowski, or Maestro as we called him, stuck rigidly to the Cecchetti Technique at class. This meant a set pattern for each day of the week.

Maestro was always neatly dressed for class in a double breasted suit and tie, and he smoked Gold Flake cigarettes throughout. Even while teaching, he'd walk round, tapping the end of his cigarette on the back of a packet, and give us the odd prod or extension to an arm. He had many good tricks to hand on: the inclination of the head, for example, towards the raised leg in a pirouette; a certain placing of the body in arabesque. But on the whole he inspired us by simply expecting good work. He never praised, but if you'd done a good class, you might be rewarded by being called over at the end of it to talk about ordinary everyday things.

"Kenya Coffee," he called to me one day, "I'd like a word with you." I ran over, pleased that I must have done well.

"Do you perhaps have any crocodile handbags you don't want?" I gulped. I did have one my aunt had given me. He must have spotted it.

"You see, I like to make things," he said, and pulled out a wallet from his pocket that was as neatly stitched and perfectly finished as I would have expected his work to be.

"Does it have to be crocodile, Maestro?" He looked at me with his eyebrows slanting down like Petrushka's, a little disappointed..... Yes, I could see – it had to be crocodile.

Madame Evina, who played the piano for class, was clearly in love with our Maestro and seldom took her eyes off him. She too had been a dancer with the Diaghilev company, and had created the child in *Boutique*. Although tiny – her feet barely reached the pedals – she was a dynamo. Her little black straw hat shook as she thumped out the chords to give Maestro a flourishing finish to one of his brilliant demonstrations of umpteen pirouettes. We whispered in the changing room about Madame Evina and her touching but hopeless love; Maestro we knew was married. Someone said she had been the original Giselle's mother and although that would have made her at least 130, it seemed plausible to us, and terribly funny.

Leslie Edwards, the well-known character dancer, told me that before the war, Ninette de Valois (later Dame Ninette) had enlisted Idzikowski to give classes at the Vic Wells Ballet in order to improve the male dancers' technique. Apparently whenever Maestro and Madame Evina entered the class room, Robert Helpmann would start humming the Pas de Trois from *Lac* under his breath and they would all get the giggles.

There were never many at his classes. In those days, class was attended by professionals only, and it was a competitive business. George Goncharov, Anna Northcote, Vera Volkova and Audrey de Vos were the fashionable teachers, and although none of them had been the dancer Idzikowski had been, for some reason he wasn't. Some thought it was his undeviating faith in the Cecchetti method. I don't suppose he minded; he believed in it. He just wasn't the fashionable sort.

Occasionally after class we'd find ourselves walking with Maestro and Madame Evina to the bus stop. If their bus came first, we'd watch them hop on like two little birds – he in his gray Homburg, long, dark coat and highly polished shoes, and she with her black straw hat, *thé dansant* clothes and highly rouged cheeks. We found it hysterical that as they pushed through to find a seat, only their hats were visible; a little black straw bobbing devotedly behind the neat gray Homburg of our Maestro – a man who in his time had partnered both Pavlova and Karsavina.

In 1957 I went to see Maestro Idzikowski with my year-old son Nic in his pram. I needed to learn a variation from Swan Lake for a comedy film I was going to choreograph. He was delighted to play with Nicolas, but when we got down to work, he became very impatient with me. I was horribly out of practice. This he completely ignored, going over every step again and again until, after two hours and gasping for breath, I finally flaked out on the floor.

"Forgive me, Maestro... I did explain... I don't have to dance this myself.... I just have to teach a small section...." I didn't add, "And then Morecombe and Wise come on and muck it all up" – it wasn't the moment. Maestro stared down at me with steely blue eyes...

Let me never forget – Stanislas Idzikowski came from the great tradition – a tradition that the eighteenth-century ballet master, Jean Georges Noverre, evoked quite simply when he wrote: "Dance is an art form difficult to acquire, and one that admits of no mediocrity."

It was Leslie Edwards, the Royal Ballet's lead character dancer, who went with a colleague to see Maestro in his London flat, shortly before he died in 1977.

"Boys," he said (according to Leslie he always called them "Boys") – "Boys, I'm very ill. I'm very ill, boys." He kept repeating it. Perhaps he thought they had come to wrap him up in a blanket and carry him off to dance.

6

LIFE IS A CABARET:
CECIL LANDAU AND THE RAJAH

By the early 1950s I had become professionally known as a dancer, and was sometimes written up in the show-biz columns. This pleased me a lot, because my dream of joining a ballet company had faded. My feet were a problem and I was never happy on pointe. The bare-foot work of Modern Ballet suited me far better – I felt free to dance, and I loved it.

When the Martha Graham-trained Bert Stimmel put on Stravinsky's *Soldier's Tale* on a Sunday night at the Whitehall Theatre, he asked me to be the Princess. This was good – a solo part. Once having stepped out of the chorus line, the hard part is to stay out of it; so I did my very best for Bert. Besides which, I had a great admiration for this American choreographer, who had taught us all the contractions, off-balance turns, knee slides, etc., that were part of the Modern Ballet vocabulary.

Crossing the stage after the show, I saw a man with a stick hobbling towards me. He said his name was Cecil Landau and that he was putting on a show at Ciro's night club. Would I be interested in joining his company? Oh yes, I would! Only £11 a week, but as the show started at midnight we would be free to do other work at the same time. *And...* there was a free supper!

In a short time I became one of Mr Landau's regulars. The others were Paddy Stone, Irving Davis, Diana Monks, Aleta Morisson and the identical Jagger twins from Guildford. We could all dance – *really* dance, and for a short time in history the show dancer got ahead of her ballet company counterpart. This was because Modern Ballet was coming over from America via American musicals. Comics and singers would be added to the cabaret according to the show and Cecil Landau's purse strings. He never stinted on a show, but his bouncing cheques were quite a feature.

Mr Landau, the king of the cabaret world, was a strange man. He had an office in Albemarle Street, and a South African girlfriend called Barbara who wore a hat, a fox fur over one shoulder, and carried a poodle. He was remote, a little grand and rightfully proud of having discovered Audrey Hepburn. He was also proud of the "good taste" of his shows, and his well known ability to pick talent.

We were never sure what form the shows would take. At the start of rehearsals we could sit around those clubs for hours, waiting for Mr Landau to turn up. When he did, he'd be rather vague, sometimes carrying books of cloth samples: "I thought this might make a nice dress for you," he'd say.

Fiz dancing with Paddy Stone, London 1955.

Slowly and surely, however, the shows would come together. The opening number of my first show at Ciro's is etched into my mind:

May I tempt you with my big red rosy apple? –
Hey there Big Boy, how about a bite?
May I tempt you with my big red rosy apple? –
Let me be your pippin for tonight.
I'll be true – I'll never be misleadin' –

We will be like Adam and Eve
Walking in the Garden of Eden.
May I tempt you with my big red rosy apple?
For yo' the apple of my eye – My, my!
Yes yo' the apple of my eye…
(*two, three, four, DANCE …*)

Years later, whenever I was going up for some tricky interview, Stanley would say, "Two quick choruses of 'Big Red Rosy Apple' and you'll be fine!"

The dance numbers I remember were "Jezebel" for Paddy Stone, Aleta and myself; "Allentown Jail," a solo for me choreographed by Frank Staff; "Let there be Love," another solo for me by Michael Charnley; and "One for my Baby," a number choreographed by Paddy Stone, which he and I danced together. They were all wonderful choreographers.

Those were the days before snobbery took a hold in the theatre, and choreographers would move easily from classical ballet to the more stimulating energy of the big musical or the intimacy of cabaret. Nothing was looked down on, and nothing was well paid. I remember Frank Staff, whose ballets "Enigma Variations" and "Peter and the Wolf" are still performed today, doing a moonlight flit because he couldn't pay the rent. He and his partner Jaquie invited me to dinner the night before leaving for South Africa. I was sworn to secrecy, which felt rather frightening.

Another of my solo numbers, this time choreographed by Beatrice Appleyard, was called "Valentine," and I danced with a big red heart on my bodice. I simply hated this dance, because it involved a lot of tricky pointe work.

There was a night when, without warning, the dance floor on which we performed had been highly polished. (No "Health and Safety" in those days). I fell – not once; not twice; but three times. On the third crash I just lay there, wishing the floor would swallow me up. Then I got up and ran off.

Mr Landau came thundering round and tore me off the most enormous strip. "You do *not* run off – you finish, somehow." I was mortified – I knew he was right. The show must go on, and on the whole we stuck to the rules: no whistling or swearing backstage; no whispering or giggling on stage; no chipped nail varnish or rings and no holes in tights. Tights were precious. We would get them invisibly mended at the cleaners. When an American gave me a pair of fish-net tights they became my most treasured possession.

During a show called *Touch and Go* we dancers were not allowed to go in or out of the stage door wearing trousers. Frocks or skirts only. It was an honour to be a part – however small – of the artistic world – and don't you forget it! Ignore the rules at your peril.

Well …

At the Washington Hotel the cabaret finished early, and the comedian Colin Croft, who lived in my direction, told me, "We can just make the midnight bus if you don't waste time taking off your makeup." We fairly flew down Half Moon Street, and got to our stop on Piccadilly with minutes to spare.

A woman approached me. "How's business, dear?" she said.

"Not too good," I replied; "but they say it will improve when the Festival of Britain begins."

She came closer. "I tell you what you do, dear. – Go down the Regent of a Friday night and order fish."

I thought the woman was mad, and looked round frantically for Colin. But he was wrapped around the bus stop sign, doubled up with laughter. Then it dawned – this was Piccadilly, not far from Shepherd's Market, the stamping ground for the Ladies of the Night.

"That'll teach you to leave your make-up on!" he said, as he pushed me onto the bus. To make matters worse, Colin told me the story of the Variety act which included two donkeys.

"One of them got his foot caught in the treadmill, and had to be shot in the interval. The other was found in the bar with his makeup on. He too was shot. You better watch it, Miss Fazan!" Colin said. And I did! I never went out in my makeup again. But I do wonder sometimes just what would have happened to me if I'd gone to the Regent Palace Hotel on a Friday night and ordered fish. And then again, if I didn't order fish …?

Part of my life at this time was a bit of a mess. I had done the classic thing of falling for a man much older than myself. Twice my age, in fact, and an out-of-work actor separated from his wife. He liked to draw and paint, and so did I. He tried to get a photography business going, and I was often forking out the little I was making to help him get started.

We never lived together – that would have been hugely shocking. But we spent time together, and I can remember having to do the weekend shopping on just half-a-crown. He and I had met in 1949 on Jack Hulbert's show; and since then I had never stopped working and moving forward. But for him it was different. He was glad to get the occasional understudy part.

While Traill was touring with the Ballet Rambert I moved into the dancer Julia Carlton's attic flat in Upper Berkeley Street where she lived with her mother. Partly to get me away from my poverty-stricken boyfriend, she was determined, she said, to "introduce me to society." Julia was perfect at the game, managing to look beautiful whatever the time of day, and laughing in all the right places. I wasn't much cop, but there was one of her aristocratic entourage – the Old Boy – who took a real shine to me. He was Sir Charles Vyner Brooke, the last white Rajah of Sarawak. He seemed to find my indifference to Julia's collection of suitors rather amusing, and that a nineteen-year-old girl without the guiding hand of parents should seem so acquiescent about moving from pillar to post, job to job, and heaven knows hand to mouth, was to him – judging from his joking astonishment – rather intriguing. Nevertheless, when Julia left the room, he made it clear to me in the kindest possible way that he would like to help me should I ever need it. I did.

In 1953 I was cast in a revue written and composed by Peter Myers, Alec Graham, David Climie, Ronnie Cass and John Pritchett. It was called *Intimacy at 8.30*. Suddenly I was being taken out by intelligent people who not only liked to laugh but were all round about my own age. I hadn't realized before what I'd been missing.

I think it took some weeks before my boyfriend realised that it wasn't just work that was keeping me away: it was *me* keeping me away. He started to bombard me with letters threatening suicide, Wills, and mementoes, and it frightened me – terrified me, in fact. My uncle Oliver came up from the country to see what he could do to help. He told me never to answer any phone calls, and to re-address all the letters "Return to Sender." Traill had got married, and I was sharing a basement flat in Cadogan Street with the dancer Maggie Pollen. One night while we were both out working, my abandoned lover broke in. After causing a great deal of disturbance, he was apparently removed in a state of disarray. Our landlord wasted no time in asking us to leave – and pronto. He needn't have worried; I couldn't wait to get out of there. And we started packing up immediately.

I rang the Old Boy. I never normally bothered him with my problems. On the contrary, I always tried to make him laugh, for he seemed to love the silly stories of our up-and-down theatre lives. But, Miracle Man that he was, he rang back to say he had arranged a flat in South Audley street for Maggie and myself to move into.

Within a day or two we were safely ensconced there, though I have to admit my nightmares continued for some time. I wonder now how I would have managed without the Old Boy's care and support. Not well, I think. He paid our rent, and all fuel bills; and the only thing I could do to show my gratitude was to lunch with him once or twice a week, or – depending on my work – go round to his house in Albion Street and amuse him with the gossip of our weekly doings.

Fiz as a South Sea Islander at London's Embassy Club. 1952.

We addressed him as "Rajah," though he was always referred to as "The Old Boy." His wife, the Ranee, lived nearby, in a flat on Hyde Park Gate, and their three daughters, who had apparently been dazzling socialites during the 1930s, now had lives of their own. Maybe the Old Boy was a little lonely. I was not the only girl he helped. There was beautiful Julia, who I'm happy to say became Lady de Saumarez, and the equally beautiful Flora, who became a Baroness. All three of us had been dancers.

One day, at lunch with the Rajah and his secretary Mrs Hussey, he said, "Do you ever hear from that tiresome boyfriend of yours?"

"No, Rajah, I don't."

"Do you know what happened to him?"

"Yes, I do. He killed himself. He put his head in a gas oven."

The Old Boy choked on his curry. His blue eyes twinkled. To him this was another funny up-and-down story of a dancer's life. To me it was horrific; something I couldn't talk about. Even now.

When the Ranee went to Barbados for the winter, she asked me to move into her flat, which I did with Joan Sims – the brilliant comedienne. We were both in *Intimacy*. She and I gave the Old Boy a party on his eightieth birthday. He sat in the armchair in the corner of the room, as though sitting on a throne, viewing us all with amusement. I hope he enjoyed himself. He didn't usually enjoy social occasions, as this letter suggests:

"This week there is an annual gathering of Sarawakians – some eighty or so – and they will come along to see me – so irksome. Why not come down Saturday evening when most will have returned home?"

He signed the letter "Rock of Ages." And well he might, for this modest, humorous, and extraordinary man had been there for me when I most needed it. How lucky is that? Very, very lucky.

But people, as people do, put their own interpretations onto things. When I first met Stanley Myers, later to become my husband, he told me that having seen our revue he had asked about me. "Oh, don't bother with her," they'd said. "Men throw themselves out of windows for her. And in any case, she's kept by a Rajah."

It shocked me. (I always felt everything was my fault.) I couldn't speak.

Stanley asked me if that was true.

"Not quite," I replied, unable to look at him.

It amazed me that he didn't seem to hold it against me. But then Stanley wasn't that sort of person.

When the Ranee returned from Barbados, the Old Boy arranged for me to move to Cheval Place in Knightsbridge. Monkey, Mr Landau's favourite girl, came to stay. She was about to marry the band leader Barry Morgan, and I was about to marry the musician Stanley Myers. Life as a Cabaret Old Chum was over for both of us. On my wedding day Monkey pinned a flower to my purse, and waved to me from the window as I trotted down the street.

I couldn't believe my own happiness, my own sense of relief.

7

GRAFT AND GRACE:
MAX RIVERS

Around the Charing Cross Road, there have always been certain dingy old office buildings that let out rooms. Some of these, with the odd mirror and barres around the walls, became the studios where we dancers took ballet class. We usually called them by their place names – West Street, or Great Newport Street – and there was always Max Rivers' Studios for rehearsal.

Apart from ballet class, there was Buddy Bradley for tap, Modern Dance with Bert Stimmel from America, Caribbean with teachers from Katherine Dunham's company, and Madame Brunelleschi for Spanish. It was a point of pride for Show dancers like myself that we should school ourselves in various styles; it was exciting too, after the shut-down of the war years, to be part of the world again. Our food became more French, and our make-up and dress more Italian. We rushed to see Roland Petit, Agnes de Mille, Ram Gopal, Antonia and Rosario, and French and Italian movies. It was a time of change, pushing us to see, hear, think and feel in a more European way. Stanley and his friends smoked Gauloise cigarettes, knew the works of Berthold Brecht and Kurt Weil, read Camus and discussed existentialism and becoming 'engagé.' Women read Simone de Beauvoir. However, there were certain British institutions that remained solidly impervious to foreign influence: Max Rivers and his studios, I should have thought, fell into this category.

The studios were rented out for rehearsals and were well known for their grime, poor changing rooms, and the musty smell of sweat and bad plumbing. We took it as a measure of the producer's budget if we were to work there: they were cheap, and it was said that Max Rivers liked to think he was helping young dancers. Very few of them knew that at the top of the dark creaking staircase Max himself sat in his dim, dingy office overlooking the Charing Cross Road, collecting the rent while the cacophony and grind of dancing feet floated up from the studios below.

Usually it was the producers who handed any money due to Max, but I once had to pay this mysterious Englishman myself. He seemed a shy and rather nervous person, jumping up from his desk and hurriedly doing up his trousers, which I presumed he had left undone in order to relieve his large paunch while reading *The Stage*. He was a cockney with a pasty moon face, and it struck me as odd that this old man, who might have seemed more at home in Berwick Market, was making his living this way, and not such a good living at that.

Looking round while he wrote out the receipt, I noticed an old sepia photograph framed on the wall. It was Max – young, svelte, and incredibly handsome in top hat and tails, dancing with the legendary Mistinguette at the Moulin Rouge in Paris. The pose they held for the photograph showed an amazing grace and style, and I, who have learnt so much from old photographs about "the way they were," knew well that it is only the rarest creatures of this world who can reveal such timeless grace in a photograph. Max Rivers smiled and muttered something when I turned to him, but he seemed not to want to talk about it, and stepped quickly back out of the light.

Some things are best left alone. But I have often wondered if Max was that young English dancing partner, Max Dearly, with whom Mistinguette fell in love. It was with him that she shocked Paris in 1910 by the daring of their new creation – the apache dance: a dance described by Josephine Baker as "a sensual series of violent attacks and caresses, that ended with them rolling on the floor."

Could it be that the modest and philanthropic Max Rivers who had danced with "La Miss" was afraid he might shock me? I shall never know.

The Charing Cross Road has been sanitized and his shabby red brick building doesn't even exist any more.

8

"SUCCESS" STORY:
DONALD ALBERY

As a young performer in musicals and variety shows I learned that the big man of the theatre was the Producer. It seemed to us that if he wasn't in his large office above some theatre, he might suddenly appear at a rehearsal or a performance, puffing away at his cigar, surrounded by devoted minions. It was clear that he called the tune and that there was little he didn't know about the theatre. In those days before subsidy and Arts Council grants, if the show didn't work you didn't eat. The Producer had to know his stuff. He might have a show running in the West End and a Number One, Number Two and even sometimes a Number Three tour of that show running simultaneously. All this has gone; killed off by the war years, television, and the rise, and rise, of the Director. The major down-side was the loss of the training these tours provided for all concerned.

However, among the Producers who survived the course in London's West End were two powerful men: Binkie Beaumont of H. M. Tennants, and Donald Albery, Sir Bronson Albery's son, of Wyndham's Theatres Ltd. Donald Albery was probably best known for his productions of *I am a Camera* ('54), *Waltz of the Toreadors* ('56), *Oliver!* ('60), and *The Severed Head* ('63).

In the autumn of 1956 *Grab Me a Gondola* opened in Windsor, at John Counsell's Theatre Royal, to much local acclaim. "The best British musical for years," they said, and "At last an answer to the Americans." These were optimistic times.

I had started as the show's choreographer, but John Counsell pushed me into directing it while he handled all administrative problems. It was of course a big break for me, although not entirely unusual in theatre terms.

In those days producers called the tune. They would normally be attached to a theatre, either through ownership or by appointment, and would sometimes handle any direction themselves. If for some reason or other they wished to hand over to a director, it was they who chose who this should be. It was an association and accepted as such. John Counsell wrote that ours "proved a most happy and fruitful arrangement."

John was very much a family man, often employing his actress wife and one or other of their two daughters.

When during our preparation I suggested my husband Stanley Myers for the position of Musical Director, John thought it a splendid idea. There were times when I had to leave my baby son and carri-cot in the girls' dressing-room, but nobody minded. The dancers spoiled him to bits. What helped me professionally – for Heaven knows direction was new to me – was that I had come straight from choreographing a Summer Season in Weymouth. In those days one would prepare three different shows to alternate throughout the summer. Apart from all the openings and finales, you had to work around comics, operatic duos, conjurers – you name it – as well as all the dance routines. It was quite a struggle to make each show different from the other.

Grab Me a Gondola – a musical – was set at the Venice Film Festival, with Denis Quilley as a *Show Page* reporter and Joan Heal as Britain's leading Film Star, alias Diana Dors. The dancers played Rank Starlets and they burst onto a sleeping Venice with a raucous opening number:

We're feeling beat and our aching feet
Don't appear to be getting us far
So grab, grab, grab me a cab
I mean grab me a Gondola....

The words were written by Julian More and the music by James Gilbert. The show had that edge of satire which was unmistakably British. The days of Revue were not yet over:

This is the place the elite meet
Film Stars and similar sweetmeat
There are lots of famous people here at Jimmy's Bar—

Ava Gardner and her Matadors meet
Eckberg and her hunk of Steele meet
And Malcolm Sargent even jives at Jimmy's Bar–

Authors who are sharp with their pen meet
John Osborne and Angry Young Men meet
Annigoni started his career at Jimmy's Bar....

A number that's essentially a list is always hell to set, but I was not to be daunted.

It was a fun time. We simply ignored the Suez crisis, and concentrated on our newly acquired continental habits. When the Starlets in *Grab Me a Gondola* go shopping it's Chianti they want:

A beautiful bottle of Vino
That's convertible into a lamp....

They say that the American insistence that the British and the French withdraw from Suez gave Britain a nervous breakdown from which it never recovered. Well, we could still laugh at ourselves. If we had fun so would the audience; and they did.

The Queen brought a party to *Grab Me a Gondola* from Windsor Castle. On stage after the performance, Her Majesty asked me seriously what it was that had made me decide to become a director. I replied, equally seriously, that I had put on so much weight while I was pregnant that I doubted anyone would employ me as a dancer. Her Majesty burst out laughing and I was fearfully pleased with myself until told later by the dancers that I had stood on one leg the entire time the Queen was speaking to me, with my other foot tucked round my knee. A bit like a comedy maid, they said. But Stanley, who watched from the wings, was really chuffed.

A few days later the West End theatre Manager Donald Albery telephoned me at home. I couldn't know this would change my life. He'd much enjoyed the show, and had arranged with John Counsell to take it over and bring it to London. He asked if I would stay on as director. *Would I?!*

The thought of the West End was such a cause for celebration that Julian More the writer, his wife Sheila, Jimmy Gilbert and his wife Fiona, Stanley and I, all went immediately to the Savoy Hotel and ordered champagne cocktails. We couldn't afford them but what the hell! This was the life....

Our benefactor, Donald Albery, after insisting on certain changes and covering himself financially with two producers whom he vigorously avoided apart from their money, was true to his word. He moved us first to the Lyric Hammersmith and then to the Lyric Shaftesbury Avenue. *Grab Me a Gondola* ran for almost two years. The show was fun, and the first to use rock music.

Donald Albery was the managing director of Wyndham's Theatres, a family concern founded by his step-grandfather, Sir Charles Wyndham, who was a powerful man. His company owned the Criterion, Wyndham's and the New Theatre; Donald himself added the Piccadilly Theatre a few years later. He presented his own productions under the banner Donmar Productions Ltd. The DON was for Donald and the MAR for Margot Fonteyn. He had formed a lasting friendship with her at Sadlers Wells. Sir Bronson Albery had placed Donald there until such time as he was considered able to take over the family empire. It was said that Donald became very bitter over the length of time Sir Bronson insisted he be trained: first as a stage-hand, then an electrician, and finally as a box-office manager. I can well imagine his impatience. He was by nature a leader.

Fearless in all his dealings, Donald saw winning as his natural inheritance. It wasn't surprising. His grand-mother, the actress Mary Moore, had successfully run the Wyndham's Theatres single-handedly after the death of her second husband, Sir Charles Wyndham, and Donald was not going to be out-shone. *The Oxford Companion to the Theatre* states that apart from being an actress of great beauty and charm, Mary Moore "retained her energy, her business acumen and her quick intelligence, to the end." The same could be written of her grandson Donald.

By his own admission, most of his time was spent as an "office boy," administering his theatres and filling them with shows from the provinces. He had a theory that only three people made any money in the theatre: the author, the successful character actor, and the theatre owner – the latter because of the rent and the bar sales. I understood that sitting in his office collecting the revenue held no appeal whatsoever for Donald. It was only when he was producing his own shows that he came into his own. No one worked harder and no one was more enthusiastic and determined to succeed than Donald himself. Producing was his life's blood.

There was only one Manager in the West End theatre who could match Donald in stature, and this was Binkie Beaumont of Tennants. Unlike Donald, Binkie did not have the power of bricks and mortar behind him. He was famous for the excellence of his products and for the charm and wit of his stars. Also for a certain subtle degree of high camp much loved by the British audience. Donald was thirty-nine before he was in a position to put on his own shows, and he wanted them to be fun: his own brand of fun. Essential to Donald's idea of enjoyment were actresses with innocence and actors who had guile and vitality.

I became part of that fun. I knew little about directing when I first worked for Donald, but I was terribly eager to learn, and nothing if not amenable. Stanley was always ambitious for me. It spurred me on and became my way of pleasing him.

Donald respected the fact that I had been a dancer – unusual in a producer, and a help for me. It mattered very much to him that I could handle comedy without going over the top. Also I was tactful – he was not – and he saw me as a useful shield; a shield against personal contact. Apart from his family and a chosen few, personal contact was something he avoided. Although I sincerely thought that Donald liked me as a person – after all when we were on tour he would wait every night to dine with me – I failed to realize how dependent that show of affection was on whether or not the show succeeded.

(Printed by permission of Ian Albery)
The producer Donald Albery.

Over a period of eight years I often dined with Donald and his wife Heather at their home in Edwardes Square. She was a charming person and hugely supportive of

Donald, but the invitations never included my husband Stanley. I brushed the hurt aside, needing the work and knowing too that the last way Stanley would want to spend an evening was by listening to endless shop and waiting until the last box-office returns had been phoned through before eating.

Donald and I would begin a production by attacking the script. "Cut the Crap" was the way Donald termed these sessions. He sat with his wooden leg up on the desk, listening intently while I read the dialogue. I never got very far before – "Cut the Crap, Whizzbang! – we've heard all this before!" Or I might shout, "Crap! – long-winded crap!" and Donald would laugh and say, "On, on, Whizzbang," before stopping me again with one of his favourites: "Unnecessary CRAP!" No explanation was needed. Our pencils scored through speech after speech until only the bare essentials of the narrative were left and the whole piece reduced to the level of simplicity Donald could tolerate. The wretched authors would then be asked to "tidy it up," and on the whole they did. Such was the power of Donald Albery in the theatre that his interest and approval generally guaranteed a play's production.

Donald was a very good-looking man, tall, elegant, and intimidating. Actors feared and disliked him as much as he avoided them. Even Noël Coward refers to Sir Bronson and Donald Albery in his Diaries as "Albery and Son – horrid Son."

During the weeks of auditions Donald would sit beside me sighing over the lack of innocence he found in each actress; or during an actor's speech he would whisper:

"Haven't I told you the most difficult part to cast in the theatre is a Gent?" Should he detect a breath of affection – he would shift uneasily in his seat and mutter under his breath, "Cringe-making, isn't it?" Donald was passionate in his convictions; he was never superior.

Once rehearsals were in progress Donald was wonderfully supportive, often bringing picnics to fuel me in the breaks, and sending me back with "On, on, Whizzbang." He needed to get the show on before the real fun could begin – the fun of the crisis. On a musical there was always a crisis, always someone Donald took wildly against and always a sacking. At first I thought he was fantastic in the way he managed to surmount the blows; but as the years rolled by I began to notice the extra glint these crises brought to his sharp eyes, his joy in the necessity of quick decision-making, his extra energy. I realised that if there hadn't been a crisis he would have created one. He attacked them to win and more often than not he did.

On *Zuleika*, his first big musical, I was brought in to replace a director who had been given the sack. The leading lady, Diane Cilento, whom Donald had found too full of guile for the part, slashed her wrists in a hotel bedroom. She wanted out, and she (and Donald?) achieved it. A young girl, whose only experience was to have swum in an Esther Williams show at Wembley Baths, was brought in as a replacement. She was "innocent," and the Press went to town. Amazingly the show almost made it – but not quite. Not all publicity was good publicity, and although the reviews were reasonable, its notoriety due to

Cilento's dramatic walk-out killed it off. Donald became more careful.

On Lionel Bart's *Blitz!*, which Lionel and I were co-directing, Donald went to endless trouble to keep the Press away. One reporter resorted to taking photographs through the skylight. He fell, injuring himself quite badly. This put an end to the hounding but not, of course, to the crises. We opened in Edmonton, a London suburb with a large theatre, and we'd meet for discussion every night after the show. At 2 a.m. one morning Lionel and Donald had an almighty row. The next day, despite our lack of sleep, Lionel and I still managed to laugh on our way to the theatre, remembering how Heather Albery had hit Lionel with her handbag. When we arrived at the theatre, however, Lionel was barred from entering. We were stunned. It wasn't going to be easy to keep rehearsals going knowing that Lionel was crouching somewhere in the gallery where he'd creep in to watch. We would phone each other at night. It was Lionel's show, and I begged Donald to reinstate him, but Donald remained adamant "for the sake of the show," and was busy replacing the choreographer. Fortunately I was in a stronger position than I knew. Donald was not prepared to tell the Press that he had given Lionel the sack and had hoped to use me as a shield. He even sent Lionel's agent to me to try to get my agreement. "You only have to say the word," the agent said, "and I'll see to it that Lionel stays away." Such is loyalty. I hung out for a very simple reason – the show needed Lionel. He was the author and composer as well. When we got to London he was back!

Blitz!, with Sean Kenny's brilliant sets, was a large and complicated production destined for the Adelphi Theatre. Donald was untiring. When we got there he sacked an entire stage crew and brought in another by the morning. *Blitz!* was well received by the critics and the public: few could dispute the enormous part Donald's driving energy had played in bringing it off. He sent me a telegram on the opening night which read: "Our love and grateful thanks for all you have done. We are enormously indebted to you as we have been so often in the past. Love from us both, Heather and Donald." I received another from Lionel which read, "From one Blitz survivor to another, love and thanks – Lionel."

Since *Grab Me a Gondola* I had directed several shows for Donald: *Paddle Your Own Canoe*, a French farce for the Criterion, the revue *One to Another*, *La Bonne Soupe* with Coral Browne, and several that Donald came in on, including the Italian show *Enrico*, *Beyond the Fringe*, and *Zuleika*. *Blitz!* was the biggest production of the lot. I proudly pasted all his messages into my scrapbook, and put them away for a rainy day. I didn't have long to wait.

Blitz!, which did well, had opened in 1962; the optimism of the 1950s had been replaced by Swinging London. My marriage was beginning to crack, and "pleasure's whirl" was fading into inconsequence.

In 1964 Donald sent me a script of a musical farce called *Instant Marriage*. It may have been a Swinging London title, but the script was awful. For the first time I turned down a job, and went on holiday with my son. When I returned the phone went: "Can you lunch with me, Whizzbang? – I've booked a table at Beotty's..." It turned out that not a single director was prepared to take on the farce, and Donald asked me if I would see him out of a jam. Partly my own loyalty to him, and partly that all too familiar and ruthless enthusiasm, beat me into submission. Brian Rix was to co-produce.

The show eventually opened out of town, again in Edmonton. I was surprised to see Lindsay Anderson in the audience. He said afterwards: "You've done all that's possible. Be encouraging– there's nothing more to do at this point." The voice of sanity. Brian Rix also had a friend out front – a farce director who had previously turned the show down, but now felt something might be done with it. Gratifying at least. The next day Donald gave me the sack and Brian Rix's friend took over.

"He said he'd like you to stay on," Donald said.

"If you don't mind, I'd much rather not," I replied; and stood up and walked away. Part of me was glad to get away and part of me was angry and frustrated that none of them could see what a struggle it had been to get the show that far. Far enough, after all, for a director who had originally turned it down to want to take it over.

It was a sad day – a very sad day for me. Donald had been such a towering force in my life; I owed him so much. And I admired him and the way he fought for his shows. He once took me to the Caprice to dine with the American director Joshua Logan. He introduced me as "the girl who listens to everyone but only ever does what she thinks best." Well, now I thought it best to leave. I hadn't succeeded. Donald withdrew his support. And that was it.

It was Max Wall, the great Music Hall comedian, who said to me when I dined with him at Rules in 1975: "You can always walk out with your head held high, you know. Oh, they'll get someone else, they always do. But," he added with one of those slow ear-to-ear grins of his, "it won't be you." I grinned too. We all learn the hard way.

As Donald would say, On, on …

Endnote: The new director on *Instant Marriage* didn't last, though whether he walked out or was pushed I've no idea. The show opened with the author directing, and was slaughtered by the Press. Lindsay Anderson sent me one of the more deadly reviews over which he'd scrawled "This is what you missed! I hope you're revitalised."

I never worked for Donald Albery again. He was knighted in 1977, changed the name of the New Theatre to The Albery and sold the family empire to a company called Maybox. Perhaps the fun was over; that passionate intensity finally quietened. Or maybe not, for he left the country with his new Japanese wife– his third – to live in Monte Carlo, where I heard he was producing shows at the Palace. He died there in 1988.

Donald's son by his first wife, Ian Albery, who had so successfully administered the family theatres, went to work for the Comedy Playhouse. Tim Albery, Donald and Heather's son, became a talented Opera director with a powerful vision of his own.

9

HIS WAY:
LINDSAY ANDERSON

I first met Lindsay Anderson in 1951 when I had just been given the dancing lead in *Touch and Go* – a show Bernard Delfont had brought over from New York to London's Prince of Wales Theatre. The show – a revue – was billed as "A Fun and Dance Show" – hence the stars: the American comedienne Kaye Ballard and three brilliant dancers, Jonathan Lucas, Helen Gallagher, whose part I was to take over, and David Lober. It was very exciting for me, as there were two serious ballets in the show, one choreographed by Helen Tamiris on a Grandma Moses theme, and the other a dramatic ballet by Hanya Holm called "Under the Sleeping Volcano"; also a comedy jive routine in a number called "A Little Bar off Times Square." At that stage of my life I was spending most of every day dancing, and I loved it. People came to see me, among them the film director Thorold Dickinson, who asked if I would test for a part in his new film *Secret People*. I was over the moon. These things seldom happen to anyone, let alone a dancer – and the part was a good one, the dancing sister of the heroine. It was arranged that I should first audition for the choreographer, and then go on to test.

Left alone on a large stage at Ealing Studios, I changed into my practice clothes and started to warm up for my chance of a lifetime. The choreographer for the film was the highly-thought-of Andrée Howard, whose ballets *La Fête Étrange* and *Lady into Fox* I had admired so much at the Ballet Rambert when my colleague and former roommate Traill, now a member of that company, could get me a ticket. I was hugely in awe of Miss Howard, and by the time she arrived I was a bundle of nerves. But she was calm and contained – and surprised, she said, by my ability to move so easily from classical ballet to modern dance. So far so good. Next I was taken to make-up, where – again to my surprise – they were all charming, and seemed to take it for granted that I had got the part. They explained that although the producer had another girl in mind, the director Thorold Dickinson had been three times to see me dance, and was determined I should play this part. (There's "another girl," I thought. Hmm...)

Make-up completed, I was taken on the set to rehearse a scene with Serge Reggiani, a French actor-singer discovered by Jean Cocteau. It may have been his part in the French Resistance during World War II that made him the perfect casting for *Secret People*. He was kind to me, but intimidating. Not able to wear my glasses, I was of necessity word perfect, but was unable to see the marks where I was to stand for the lights. By the time they were ready to shoot, I was shaking from head to foot. That over, and not well done, someone was delegated to take me to the café before the make-up test.

That someone was Lindsay Anderson. He sat me at a table in the canteen and returned with two mugs of tea and two custard tarts. I hate custard tarts, but this man had such a masterful air of authority about him that I ate mine in one, just to please him.

He explained that he was attached to the unit in order to write something about the making of the film. Shuffling among his papers, he got out a notebook and pen, and asked, "What does it feel like to be suddenly given a star part in a movie?"

Did I detect a faintly mocking edge, or was it just me? Anyway, I had no means of dealing with it, and answered truthfully, "I don't believe I've got it."

Nor had I. The "other girl" got it. Her name was Audrey Hepburn.

Nine years later, and much water under the bridge, I had a telephone call from Oscar Lewenstein. Would I go to his office to meet Lindsay Anderson, who was to direct *The Lily White Boys* (a play written by Harry Cookson with songs by Christopher Logue and Tony Kinsey) for the Royal Court? It needed some choreography.

I had just directed a revue called *One to Another* with Disley Jones as designer and my husband Stanley Myers as composer and musical director. We had collected material – both sketches and songs – from all over the place. The contributors included Serge Gainsbourg, John Mortimer, Harold Pinter and the wonderful N. F. Simpson. Not one of the many authors we contacted asked for up-front money. Those were the days! They were rewarded however by receiving glowing reviews – Pinter's first.

One to Another was the sixth show I had directed in the West End, but like most people I know in the theatre, you are always convinced that every job will be your last. It's funny to remember that around this time the director Peter Brook remarked to Julian More that to succeed as a director in the theatre one must either form one's own company like Peter Hall and build an Empire, or have private money.

"He doesn't think you'll make it," Julian told me.

"Really?" I said, reeling. "Why not?"

"Because you have neither."

Too true! I was never a "career" person: I didn't pick and choose, I just took the next job. Stanley taught me that it was best to do everything, be it a jingle for a TV advert or something for the concert hall. "It's all music," he'd say. "Where's the problem?" I agree. It's all tap dancing.

I was very pleased to have that telephone call from Oscar Lewenstein, whatever the offer. Just to be asked to work at the Royal Court at that time was a huge honour. Since 1956 and John Osborne's *Look Back in Anger*, it had been viewed by the outside world as an exclusive enclave for the writers, artists and intellectuals of the day. The standard of productions there was exciting and new. I scraped my hair back, dressed in the simplest garb, and set off. Lindsay made a faint effort to put on his shoes as I walked in, and shook my hand. We talked of my show. Oscar liked it, but Lindsay clearly didn't.

"What do *you* think of it?" he asked me; and I sensed again that particular edge of mockery and expectation. (Will she come up with something?)

"I think bits of it are very good," I carefully replied.

Lindsay sniffed. (That's not good enough: far too trite.)

But a script was handed to me and an appointment made to meet at the Royal Court in a few days. This time I put on my red dress (leftish), and I can remember wondering if Lindsay was Polish, with his leather cap and jacket. He showed me the stage, explained the set, and then took me to the bar upstairs. There they all were – the intellectuals – casually discussing the state of the world. Lindsay introduced me around. Some knew of me, though I knew none of them. Then what I most dreaded might happen — did happen! George Devine, the founder with Tony Richardson of The English Stage Company and artistic director at the Royal Court, took his pipe out of his mouth and turned to me.

"And what is your opinion of Brecht, Miss Fazan?" In the silence that followed I wanted to die. Was "brecht" a method, or some play I should have seen but hadn't? Bang goes this job, I thought. There was nothing for it...

"I'm afraid I don't know anything about it," I replied.

"Well, that's a relief," said Lindsay; and they all laughed. Saved – and not for the last time – by the man who was to become my staunchest friend and my bulwark against the slings and arrows.

That afternoon Stanley and I were rehearsing a cabaret act for Graham Payne at the Café de Paris. I told Graham what had happened at the Royal Court, and he later told Noël Coward. The Master was most amused. "I bet that took her Brecht away," he said.

As soon as he could Lindsay took me to a corner to discuss the script of *The Lily White Boys*. I told him I thought there was a problem with the closing of the first half. It was too final. "You must leave the audience wanting to know what happens next."

"So what do you think should happen?"

"Well, they could finish the number, and on the play-out Albert yells, 'Let's go, lads!' and they run greedily up the stairs as you bring the curtain down. That will bring the audience back. They'll want to know where the hell they got to."

Lindsay threw back his head and roared with laughter. (Circumspect and unashamedly commercial.) He put his hand on my shoulder. And said, "I think you and I will get on very well."

And we did. Amazingly so. Lindsay's mind functioned so far above my own, yet he seemed genuinely interested in what I had to say rather than just what I did. Luckily for me he was very suspicious of any intellectual approach, and there was no fear of that with me. We enjoyed going to things together – film or theatre – where he'd whisper questions like "Well, how's it going?" or "What do you think?" And if he didn't like it – "Is it always like this?" – followed by an enormously long and loud sigh; and in the interval, "Feel like a curry?" Though woe betide anyone who left at the interval during one of *his* plays!

Neither of us had been born in England, and both of us were children of divorced parents. Divorced in the days when the world's disapproval was all too apparent. We never talked about it – we wouldn't have; but once when I went to visit him I saw that he had *Who's Who* open on his desk.

"My father is in there," I said.

"So is mine," he countered.

While Lindsay was out of the room making coffee I glanced down at the entries, and there he was – Major General Anderson. But where my father had recorded both his marriages and all offspring, the Major General mentioned only his second marriage. It was as if Lindsay, along with his mother and brother Murray, had never existed. I closed the book before he returned.

Watching Lindsay rehearse was an education for me. He created an easy but strong working atmosphere – discussing and laughing a good deal without ever losing sight of where he was heading. Things that I'd held dear, like my professionalism and my ability to suspend disbelief and dedicate myself to whatever – were not wanted here. It was the individual approach, and having a point of view, that were important.

"She's very professional" I soon learnt was no compliment. Lindsay once wrote to me: "I am endeavouring to tread the narrow path between commitment (whole-hearted) and detached opportunism (i.e. being 'professional') Not easy... but so far I'm managing."

Director Lindsay Anderson at work 1980s.

Actors loved Lindsay. His intelligence, humour and empathy made them feel secure. After rehearsal he'd put on his duffle coat and cap and go to the pub with the actors. I had been schooled by Donald Albery to keep a distance between myself and the actors, no doubt in order to retain authority. This was not Lindsay's way. To him there was only "Them" and "Us." The "them" that would never understand and the "us" who did!

Apart from choreographing the numbers, I helped out wherever I could. I asked Lindsay round to make a list of all the lighting cues required. This was something I was used to. Only the big producers with big shows hired a lighting designer, and even then it was usually the production manager. On the smaller shows that I'd been involved with it was the set designer, the director, stage-manager and chief electrician who sorted out the lights. So I was surprised to see Lindsay wandering off to talk to the actors in the middle of the lighting rehearsal, leaving me to give out the cues and their timing. George Devine wrote me a letter: "I do appreciate *how much* you have done for this show – way beyond the limits of your precise function …" Limits? We didn't do limits where I came from.

The Lily White Boys opened in January 1960, with the young Albert Finny and Georgia Brown as the stars. The critics were grudging. "Rough night with the Cosh Boys," they called it. "A fine old time bashing the Establishment and the Establishment seeming quite to enjoy it." Well, some did, some didn't. And although Lindsay's direction was praised as "deft, unfussy and direct," the play wasn't a resounding success.

"It's beyond human ability to create a just society" was a line in Christopher Logue's *Lily White Boys*. It might have been written by Lindsay himself. He enjoyed a bit of world-weary fatalism. "Oh, well, Fiz, what can you expect?" – followed by: "You didn't expect them to be NICE, did you?"

One didn't use the word "nice" in Lindsay's presence, and nor did one use "one." Too genteel for a person who had fought the Class War all his life. Rather stupidly I once told him I was vague on the subject of class, having been brought up in Africa where people were either white or black. "Well, don't expect to work in this country without knowing all there is to know about Class," Lindsay said, and I was suitably quashed.

He did his best to educate me. He bought me *War and Peace* and Stevie Smith poems. He took me to John Ford's and André Vajda's movies, and he always came to whatever I was doing. When I was on tour I'd sometimes see him sitting in the stalls all by himself, ready to discuss it afterwards.

"Be more like Bette Davis," he'd say to me. Or "Perhaps you need a dose of feminism."

I told him that an analyst had once advised me to have a cutting remark up my sleeve, to produce every time someone was horrid to me – the idea being that it stops them from ever doing it again.

"I like the sound of that man," Lindsey said. "Come, let's practice. Try 'Piss off, you little fart!'"

We were dining in a restaurant with Frank and Ginette Grimes. "Piss off, you little fart," I said.

"No, no, no! – much louder – more conviction. Like this." He turned his head as though someone was standing behind him. "Oh, piss off, you little fart!" – and turned back as though ignoring them. I started to laugh, and so did the whole restaurant. Lindsay was famous for his cutting remarks. He was a man of great insight and perception, but oh boy, he knew how to lash out.

His work often took him abroad, either directing or promoting a movie, and I have cards from him from all over the world. We all did. Often written in red ink, and seldom without his particular brand of critical examination:

"I've gone right off New York this time … I can't stand their corrupt super-triviality. Broadway is so scruffy you can't really worry about it …"

"Script conferences started last week: GORE VIDAL *not* the most stimulating of collaborators – being snobbish and vain as well as intelligent. How lovely to be so happy to be invited to dinner by Harold [Pinter] and Antonia!"

"Have just managed to hold [Claudette] Colbert and [Rex] Harrison in balance. Both monsters in their egotistical way. She is a ball-breaker and he a virtuoso egomaniac. Both performers rather than actors."

"Our friends the critics have no indulgence except for the fashionable."

"Vanessa [Redgrave] arrived in a particularly sulky, broody, self-righteous, revolutionary mind (England a police state, etc.) and finally turned on me quite savagely as a callous, complacent reactionary, whereupon I rose without a word and left. Tony [Richardson] followed apologetically and drove me home. I was tempted to feel sorry for him."

"I'm no Shakespeare director, not in England that is. You can't buck Peter Hall and the RSC with impunity. Well, fuck 'em."

"I think Rachel made me feel how impossible it was to help people. Must struggle against this. 'Say not the struggle naught availeth.' See you soon. Love, L"

And he was just as outspoken in interview. "His bitterness cost him his career," John Schlesinger said to me one evening. But I never saw it that way. Lindsay believed in the artist's right – duty, almost – to criticize. He was brave about voicing his critical beliefs even when it compromised his chances of future work. This was noble, because underneath – though he would never admit this – there was nothing he wanted more than that the National or the RSC should invite him to do a production. He was an artist and he needed to work. I think he hoped that a producer who believed in him and his work would surely come along one day, but it never really happened.

Because Lindsey seldom needed a choreographer, this story is more about our friendship than about being colleagues. When he did need a choreographer, happily he would employ me. I worked on two Christopher Logue plays for him at the Royal Court, two different *Cherry Orchards*, and a Players scene for his Frank Grimes *Hamlet*. As he loved to end his works on a jolly note, I also arranged various musical finales for him – quite an elaborate one for *The Bed Before Yesterday*, during which he gave me what can only be described as a hard time. I put this down to the fact that during my rehearsals I had to take charge, and Lindsay found that difficult to stomach. Also he had done such a brilliant and witty job on the direction I didn't think it needed a big finale, and said so. Big mistake!

When Helen Mirren wanted to change a sequence of steps to something I thought pretty naff, I said, "We can easily change it – that's not the problem: it's just not quite as good." Whereupon Lindsay jumped up from the stalls and said, "We will do it Helen's way, whether you like it or not." His actors always came first! I kept going – one always does. But as soon as the first preview was over I telephoned Lindsay at home and explained that Scottish Opera was waiting for me, and if he didn't need me any more, rather than hanging around for the opening night I should like to go. There was silence at the end of the phone. Lindsay was dumbfounded. He was not about to say that I was needed in any way; but that someone wouldn't want to be there for the opening night – that was incomprehensible to him. The fun, the nerves, the dressing-room drinks and friends – Lindsay loved all that. Beastly me was glad to get away. When I returned a few weeks later, there was a message asking if I would take some understudy calls. There at the stage door was a Christmas present for me from Lindsay. The attached card had a picture of a little girl sitting up in bed, evidently rather sick. The caption read:

I send this token that it may bear
A wealth of love, of wishes true,
And a simple earnest prayer
That silently goes up for you!

In 1973 Lindsay asked me to choreograph his movie *O Lucky Man*, and to sit beside him as his casting director in the final scene where he played himself – the director of the film. I noticed that his ears were very pink; he was dreading his part in the scene. During the lunch break we hid behind a lorry on the lot to go through it time and time again. I remember thinking what a huge strain it must be for this very kind-hearted, highly astute, but rather uncertain person to be always Lindsay Anderson: a man ever scornful of bullshit and celebs. He had to show them.

I could list a thousand examples of Lindsay's kindness – his genuine interest in people's endeavours, his care for those in trouble; the birthday parties he gave for his niece and nephew; the cheque he sent me when I'd done some unpaid work for him, with the note, "I hope you won't be too proud or too bourgeois to accept the enclosed"; his coming down to Brighton to help me when I was floundering as an actress, unable to be heard beyond the front row of the stalls. He took me out after the show and made me shout from the Brighton esplanade, while he stood on the shingle in the dark getting sprayed by the waves. We all have these memories of Lindsay's kind heart and his willingness to put himself out for others.

But there was a tricky side to him. I saw it once very clearly, and it shook me. I had directed the Alberts, the crazy and gifted brothers – Tony and Douglas Gray with Bruce Lacey and various friends – in *The Three Musketeers* at the Arts Theatre. It was mostly panned by the press, but Lindsay loved it, and booked us to be the Christmas show at the Royal Court. Rachel Roberts was to play Madame de Winter, with the kindly dark-voiced Valentine Dyall as Cardinal Richelieu. By the time we came to rehearse,

Rachel was in the midst of her very painful break-up with her husband Rex Harrison. We got through rehearsals pretty well – I think Rachel was glad to be working. If for any reason I had to keep her waiting, Valentine Dyall would take her off to the pub round the corner. As far as I remember, we opened a few days before Christmas to excellent reviews all round; but on Christmas Day Lindsay telephoned to say that Rachel had taken an overdose and was in hospital. Would I get the understudy on for Boxing Day?

A couple of days later he telephoned again to say Rachel would be on that night, and that he and I should greet her at the theatre as there would be photographers about. As we waited on the pavement, Rachel arrived in a taxi with a nurse and a girl friend. Suddenly I saw Lindsay heave himself forward, violently pushing people out of the way in the most ruthless manner, until he was beside Rachel, and they could together turn to the photographers. It horrified me. My hero, who, despite all that he stood for, had such a desperate need to be Centre Stage, to be King of the Castle. I thought at the time that it smacked of some colossal vanity.

I was wrong. Nothing about Lindsay could be that simple. Lawrence Joseph, in his book on *Character and Self-Expression*, seems nearer the mark when he says that the Narcissist creates a public image which he believes to be his true self. His real personal self becomes irrelevant to him – even inconsequential. This might explain Lindsay's celibacy. Long ago Jocelyn Herbert, the brilliant designer and George Devine's partner, told me that Lindsay had admitted to her that he'd never felt the need for any sexual gratification. I took that to be the truth, as she did; if it didn't matter to him, it didn't matter to us. It is true of course that much of Lindsay's spare time and energy went into furthering the careers of certain young actors – Albert Finney, Tom Courtney, Richard Harris, Alan Bates, Malcolm McDowell, and Frank Grimes all benefited. Although his (posthumously printed) diaries reveal some masochistic fantasies about Richard Harris, I always felt it was the relationship that mattered to him: the master-pupil relationship and rather paternal in its way – something Lindsay had never had himself. It mattered to him to support the individual talents of his profession. Had he lived long enough to hear himself dubbed a homosexual, I doubt he would have given a damn. There would be that ironic shrug and "Surely, Fiz, you've learnt by now it's the way of the world."

Okay – yes, but I was still surprised to hear David Storey, Lindsay's great friend and collaborator, say on the radio that Lindsay's homosexuality informed all his work. Sorry, I don't agree. It was the human struggle – in all its forms, though mainly against the powers that be – that informed Lindsay's work. You see it – in *This Sporting Life, If, In Celebration, O Lucky Man, The Whales of August* – everywhere. Even in an early film I can remember a little provincial Lord Mayor hilariously plodding across a field in all his regalia, late for some function but clinging at all costs to his dignity. Lindsay's work was nearly always humorous and affectionate, with an unmistakable irony that gave it an edge.

Not long ago I was taken by Anthony Page to a special showing of the film Lindsay made for the pop group WHAM during their tour of China. WHAM refused to allow it to go out, and you can see why! It's not a put-down exactly, for there are plenty of screaming Chinese fans and fawning diplomats, but the concert and its preparation are set against the profundity of the Chinese aesthetic, the inscrutable river-boat people and the landscape of the East, which Lindsay and his cameraman had clearly found very beautiful. The irony of the contrast with the very Western pop concert said everything!

I have another picture of Lindsay that has stuck in my mind. I had twice choreographed the family dance for him in *The Cherry Orchard* – once at Chichester with Celia Johnstone and the second time with Joan Plowright at the Haymarket Theatre. Lindsay had hoped to bring out the comedy in Chekhov. I was not there for the opening, having had to leave after the first preview to work abroad. When I returned Lindsay mentioned that the reviews had been mixed – some of them vituperative.

"That old wish to bring me down. Others disliked the production."

"What did they want?" I asked. "Did they say?"

Lindsay wrinkled up is nose: "They want to be *moved*," he said with contempt. "One critic seemed dismayed that Madame Renevsky seemed to *want* to leave the cherry orchard. Well, yes. She wants to return to her lover. She does say she loves him in Act II. Human nature. Chekhov was a realist – but that's not what they want." He was depressed. "I think if I didn't know it was the way of the world it *would* bring me down."

He'd arranged a seat for me for the last night. At the end, after a couple of company calls, Lindsay strode cheerfully onto the stage, followed by the stage manager carrying trays of vodka. Glasses were handed out to the company on stage, and then Lindsay turned to the audience and asked us all to join him in a toast. Holding his glass of vodka he strode down to the front of the stage, raised it to the gallery – or "the Gods," as we term it – and called out "To Chekhov!" While he stood there in silence, arm raised, the curtain descended.

As the audience shuffled away, somewhat bemused it has to be said, I sat there hard pushed to move. Lindsay was such a brave man; at that moment it seemed as if "the human struggle" was all his own.

"Now then, Fiz – don't get sentimental – that's far too easy. Some gleeful malice is what we need from you!"

Lindsay's last years were tough. He was ill prepared for being no longer in demand. He had two projects that he really cared about, both written by David Sherwin – one of them a sequel to *If* – but they never got off the ground. And the critical failure of *Britannia Hospital* hit him very hard. I remember his dismay when Stephen Daldrey, the artistic director of the Royal Court, told Lindsay he was considering putting on *The Contractor*, a David Storey play successfully directed by Lindsay some years previously. "Do you know, he didn't even mention the possibility of my directing it." Sad. Somewhere he had lost his ability to give an ironic shrug to the new broom sweeping clean. He saw it as indifference.

Lindsay's heart started to go wonky. Where we used to go out and about, I now drove round to his place in Swiss Cottage. There would always be a collection of videos to watch: old musical comedy films that we both loved – Lindsay every bit as much as I. We'd compare the British and American styles – the Black influence and the lack of it in Britain, or how musicals dealt with the Depression, and we'd sit happily for hours. Lindsay had a very good singing voice, and sometimes as I was leaving – clatter clatter down those stairs – I would hear him singing at the top. Often the Vivian Ellis song:

Even when the darkest clouds are in the sky,
You mustn't sigh
And you mustn't cry.
Just spread a little happiness
As you
      go
        by...

10

THE NORTHERN STAR IN PANTO: GEORGE FORMBY

For Christmas 1960, I was to direct a pantomime for Harold Fielding at the Bristol Hippodrome. It was to be *Aladdin,* and George Formby was to play Mr Wu the Chinese Laundry Man. I got there on Sunday, December 11th, with just two to weeks to rehearse before opening on Christmas Eve.

Quaking somewhat, I was taken by Mr Fielding to meet the Star in his dressing room.

George Formby was a Lancashire comic with a ukulele. He had started his career in the Music Hall in 1921, and had risen to become a huge star with a film contract worth £100,000 by 1938. He played a gormless young man with a wide, toothy grin, much loved as "the small-town twerp with dreams of glory." It was a part from which he never deviated; it suited the depression years of the '30's, and George was no fool. "He was the tops," they said, and his songs "brought happiness to everyone." They had titles like "When I'm Cleaning Windows," "If I'd Biceps, Muscle and Brawn," and "Count Your Blessings and Smile." He had been a great favourite during the war, travelling extensively with his wife Beryl between films, giving troop concerts wherever he could.

I smiled as I was introduced to George Formby – he looked rather dour, I thought. Harold Fielding counted his blessings, as he left us discreetly alone.

"Are you happy with the way Mr Wu has turned out?" I started off – script in hand. He grinned – that huge, toothy grin, and looked me up and down.

"By gum" he said, "but you're a lucky lass our Beryl's not here," and calmly pinched my bottom.

"I do need to discuss your final spot," I gulped. "You've probably seen it's left blank in the..."

"She'd have your guts for garters, Beryl would." (Pinch, pinch.)

"OW... yes, I heard your wife was ill. I was sorry to..."

"Don't be sorry, lass. (Large leer.) You don't know Beryl like I do. She'd take one look at you and you'd be out on your (pinch, pinch). Eee, but she'd see to that. She's hard, our Beryl; hard as nails. I've suffered that. She won't so much as let a woman look at me. You can thank your lucky stars Beryl's not here, she'd have your guts (pinch) for garters." (Pinch, pinch.)

(Hulton archive/getty images)
George Formby as everyone knew him. 1944.

Feeling anything but lucky, and by now backed up against the wall, I was saved by a knock at the door. A man from the *Bristol Evening News* had arrived to interview Mr Formby.

"Please come in; I'm just going," I said, opening the door, and turning to George. "We can find some other time to go through your final spot." He winked at me, and I knew I was in for a bumpy ride. Beryl might be a trial, but she had her uses.

The next day there was a big article in the newspaper: the tears behind the face of the clown. George Formby's devastation that his wife Beryl could not be with him, due to her illness; but like every good trooper, he would hide his grief and carry on. The public must only guess at the anguish behind that famous smile...

Not until years later did I find out that Beryl had indeed kept him in a strait jacket. She was a tap dancing comedienne when George met her in 1920, and was responsible for his becoming a Music Hall entertainer. They were married in 1924. Many people thought that George owed much of his success to Beryl's ruthless ambition, and that he was afraid of her. George's co-stars had been crisply laundered girls-next-door: Florence Desmond, Googie Withers and Phyllis Calvert. Phyllis Calvert, speaking recently on TV, said that knowing George's reputation with the ladies, she had been almost put out that he hadn't seemed to notice her; but as soon as Beryl left – he did!

It was the wonderful Valentine Dyall – our Abanazar in *Aladdin* – who asked me towards the end of our rehearsal time if the gossip had been true: that "George was always trying to get you on your own."

"It's possible," I admitted, and told him of that first encounter. To my surprise Valentine roared with laughter. "I don't know why, but I always think of you arriving from Africa in a straw hat with a daisy sticking up on top." I wasn't really such an innocent little thing. But from a child I had been told it was your fault should a man make a pass at you: you had in some way "led him on." Even at the age of thirty I still thought it best to shut up. I still felt ashamed.

George didn't rehearse, I discovered; he walked it – just the exits and entrances and a few production numbers. The cast, who would have liked to know what he was up to, disliked him intensely. They just gave up on him and got on with the show. It was a large and lavish production. We never did discuss that final spot – just the light cues and the order for the band.

George Formby Senior, George's father, had been a favourite Music Hall artist before him, one of the only two Marie Lloyd said she would watch from the wings – the other was Dan Leno. Unable to get rid of the bronchial condition he'd contracted as a young blacksmith, he incorporated his cough into his act, frequently stopping in the middle of a song to remark: "Coughin' summat champion toneet." This saying became his touching trademark. His son, George Formby Junior, had another – "It's turned out nice again." And indeed it did for him. He was a British working-class Star with all that went with it at the time: wealth, a palatial mansion outside Blackpool, a white Rolls Royce, and above all, every audience in the palm of his hand.

When we opened on Christmas Eve the show was fine but George was fantastic – his final spot, just a front cloth, was by far the best thing in the show.

The Bristol Hippodrome is a large theatre, but they cheered him to the roof tops, and wouldn't let him go. He was grand, there is no doubt about that, and I too was hoarse from cheering, for I love this sort of theatre more than any other. Just a ukulele, the monstrous grin, and all the old favourite songs. He didn't need anything else.

"One more for Beryl," they shouted from the gallery...
I'm leaning on a lamppost at
The corner of the street in case
A certain little lady comes by.
Oh me, oh my,
I hope that little lady passes by.
She said that she would get away
She doesn't always get away
But anyhow I know that she'll try...

Note: Beryl died a few weeks later. George made a bid for a new life by becoming engaged to a young teacher, but he died soon afterwards in 1961, aged fifty-six.

11

BEYOND THE FRINGE: ALAN BENNETT, PETER COOK, JONATHAN MILLER, DUDLEY MOORE

Peter Cook, Jonathan Miller, Alan Bennett and Dudley Moore had been brought together by a mutual friend – John Basset – to put on their own show at the Lyceum Theatre in Edinburgh. They called it *Beyond the Fringe*, and it was a triumph.

Jonathan Miller was a young doctor aged twenty-six; Alan Bennett, also twenty-six, a medieval historian at Oxford; Peter Cook, twenty-three, was already writing for revue; and Dudley Moore, twenty-five, was a jazz musician. They all had Oxbridge in common: Peter and Jonathan were from Cambridge and the Footlight revues, and Alan and Dudley came from Oxford and the

Experimental Theatre Club. They went into show business for "the laughs and the money," and they became the sacred cows they had set out to satirize. It isn't easy working with sacred cows.

With the enormous success of *Beyond the Fringe* in Edinburgh, Peter's agent, Donald Langdon, was able to make a deal with his friend William Donaldson for a London production. Donaldson (or "Willie") was an independent theatre producer aged twenty-three with whom I had worked before – called in on a floundering revue that never made it past Oxford. Now he phoned to ask if I would see *Beyond the Fringe* into London. The show was a proven success, Willie explained, so it would be a small job: a sort of umpire-cum-production manager with a fixed salary of £10 a week. He realised I would need to see the show before making any decision, and had arranged for a performance in a London rehearsal room. He didn't add that he hadn't seen the show either.

I was curious and very interested to see the four of them. They were extremely funny and a lot of their material, which satirized conventions – particularly the class-orientated Britain of the time – was witty and original. And they wrote their own material. I could well understand their personal success, but the show was badly put together, and their attitude was typically undergraduate. To reach any sort of London standard they would have to work hard; I wondered if their rebellious spirit, which was a valuable part of the show, could tolerate hard work. I doubted it, and told Willie of my misgivings: some of the material would have to go, and as the show was only an hour long, a great deal more written. It was going to be a huge job.

(Popperfoto/getty images)

Peter Cook, Jonathan Miller, Dudley Moore and Alan Bennett in "Beyond the Fringe" 1961

Willie was delighted. He'd had his misgivings too and had been afraid that I might have found *Beyond the Fringe* as wonderful as everyone else. On the basis of this understanding I agreed to take on the job. No extra money, of course. There was none.

Rehearsals for the London show had to wait some months, as Peter Cook had been asked by Michael Codron to write some sketches for a revue he was doing with Kenneth Williams, and both Dudley Moore and I had prior commitments. Willie came to see me. He was having difficulty in getting a London theatre interested in booking the show. Not surprising. However successful a show may be on the Edinburgh Fringe, it does not guarantee a London theatre. He asked if I would help him persuade Donald Albery to join us. I had already directed three London revues: the last, *One to Another*, was with Donald as producer. Once he'd struck a hard bargain with Willie, Donald agreed to come on board. This was good news.

John Basset warned me that the quartet was impossible to work with: "You'll never get them to rehearse," he said.

"I have one minimal requirement," I said to them on the first day of work: "Turn up." I think they were so surprised, they always did.

That first week was spent in my flat exploring new material with a tape recorder and Willie's secretary to get it down onto paper. We worked every day from 10 to 5.30, and I don't think I've ever laughed so much – their rivalry spurred them on, and the poor secretary didn't know what had hit her.

Peter was invariably the instigator of the ensemble ideas; Jonathan with his lolloping charm would leap to his feet and perform, while Alan held his own and Dudley seemed bewildered. Ideas and witticisms poured out of Peter in never-ending supply. He was a giver, using a rather superior and casual front to hide his sensitivity. Alan was cautious; he stuck to his own judgement, and was extremely funny and courteous. Lines about Cliveden and the foibles of upper-class speech would be his; the issue of class both fascinated and amused him. Jonathan, always anxious that giving up medicine might prove to have been a mistake, thought visually. His considerable imagination gave him, as it often seems to, a natural sense of history. He was the most humane and the most enthusiastic.

Dudley wanted everything to be jokey and friendly. Perhaps it hid his lack of confidence. He found work difficult – almost agonising. He would sit at the piano unable to make any decisions, despite his extraordinary musical talent, and it was Jonathan who helped him to get his solos together. It wasn't surprising, some twenty years later, to see Dudley on TV in New York still performing the identical pieces he'd fixed in my flat. Only a star can get away with that. As for myself, I was four years their senior, and had been working for twelve years without the help of much education other than what some people are pleased to call "Life's" (some people – not me!).

At the end of that first week, John Wyckham, our lighting designer and chosen by Donald, came over to discuss the show's format with me. We drew out a set of rostra on my kitchen floor. This was to be our set – not much liked by the quartet, but it gave the show some visual variety – and John arranged via Donald Albery to have it ready for our rehearsals in the bar at the Prince of Wales Theatre.

As long as the enthusiasm kept up, the Oxbridge four worked extremely hard in rehearsal – but only when we were alone. Should anyone pass through, even a cleaner, they would immediately start mucking about. To be caught working was more than their English education would allow, and God forbid that they should be taken for actors in need of instruction. Meanwhile I had to get the show right.

At our technical rehearsal, which the quartet slumped and mucked their way through, John Wyckham turned to me and said: "I don't know how you can stand it." But by that time, I was able to reply: "It's only an act; they're very ambitious really." I knew, too, that "Stop this unprofessional behaviour" would have been music to their ears. They were going to succeed because they were NOT professional – they were brilliant.

We opened in Cambridge with still plenty of work to do. We rehearsed all day, and I changed the running order for every performance until it seemed right. The show was bound to go well with the university audience – which didn't help. But I think that by then all four of them were pleased to have me there to bear the brunt of their individual frustrations, if nothing else. There was still more rivalry between them than friendship, and removing solo spots was a tricky and delicate task. Alan Bennett seemed to have hundreds. In the way they each fought for their own spots, they were no different from any revue artist I'd ever worked with. Not that I said so.

Donald Albery had booked the show into Cambridge and Brighton, but had so far failed to secure a London theatre. Willie was a very shy man and left it to me to ask Donald Albery if he would come down to see *Beyond the Fringe* in Cambridge.

Donald came with his wife Heather. He wasn't very enthusiastic. The show was too consciously "knowing" for his brand of fun, and he spent most of the time over supper bemoaning the state of the theatre.

"I think you'd have fun with this one, Donald," I said, knowing how to wait my moment. I don't think he believed me. We went on to Brighton in pretty good shape but with no London opening in sight.

Brighton didn't take to the show. The reviews were bad to meagre, and the audience poor. Far more worrying was the fact that we had nowhere to go on to. Momentum is very important; particularly with hardened unprofessionals.

I asked Lindsay Anderson to come down and lend support. I'd grown fond of all four of them, and knowing their confidence had taken a bit of a knock in Brighton, I thought Lindsay would boost it. I got it wrong. After a brief introduction, the four quite positively fled out to supper leaving Lindsay and his support rejected in the wings. It was their show and was going to remain so. Having instigated the whole thing, I searched for some excuse. "They're not interested, Fiz – it doesn't matter," Lindsay said, and wrinkled up his nose. "They're certain to be a huge success anyway."

The next day Donald Albery phoned to say that he had arranged for Anna Dere Wyman, the managing director of London's Fortune Theatre, to see the show in Brighton. "Look after her," he said. "Do what you can."

Anna Dere Wyman brought her solicitor, and we all met up after the show in the little backstage bar known as The Single Gulp. Miss Wyman was already drunk. It was all we needed. After various attempts at communication and a few jokes, the quartet got fed up and left me to it. I didn't blame them. The only thing that seemed to interest Miss Wyman, apart from the vodka, was the fruit machine. She dispatched me every few seconds to put in the shillings since she was too wobbly to do it herself. Pulling the handle on about the tenth shilling, and watching the lemons and pears whizz round, I suddenly thought, What the Hell am I doing? I like this show.... I excused myself and returned to my hotel defeated. Fortunately her solicitor had enjoyed the evening, and on the Saturday Donald phoned to say we were in business.

Beyond the Fringe opened at the Fortune Theatre in May 1961. The rest is history. Standing room only until the celebrated four left for New York to take Broadway by storm. History in more ways than one, for with the onset of the Beatles and rock music, revue rapidly disappeared. *That Was The Week That Was* reclaimed revue on TV, where it has remained: still topical, still witty, but lacking the intimacy of a small theatre and the resulting sense of sophistication, fun, even glamour, felt by an intimate revue audience which, for two hours, was in on a satire of London's contemporary events.

It was Alex Cohen who first put in a bid for the New York production of *Beyond the Fringe*. Donald Albery immediately telephoned David Merrick, Cohen's most powerful rival on Broadway, and forced them to bid against each other. The price soared to such an extent that Alex Cohen, who won the contest, took my director's credit for himself in order to get the percentage. The brilliant quartet were at least put on decent salaries. They and Donald agreed that it was only proper that my £10 a week should continue with a further £10 from New York.

Some time later I was asked to go over to put in some new numbers. "You've never been to New York," Donald said. "It will be a treat for you."

Jonathan met me at the airport and drove me to the theatre. I felt very lucky, but rather apprehensive and alone. The darlings of Broadway had become so charming, and so confident of their talents, that I hardly knew them.

During the London run, Peter Cook had started the magazine *Private Eye*, and opened a club in Soho called *The Establishment*, to which London flocked. It was a place where his friends could work. The cabaret, a little reminiscent of Berlin thirty years before, was always intelligent; sometimes brilliant.

Dudley Moore later became a Hollywood film star; Jonathan Miller a hugely respected opera and theatre director as well as a media personality; Alan a successful playwright and much-loved TV writer; and Peter Cook, always the least personally resolute, a cult figure emulated and admired by every satirical writer worthy of the title. None though could match his immaculate sense of timing.

It seems incredible that these sought-after men started out simply "for the laughs and the money" – but that's what they said.

They – not me!

12

"CAVATINA":
STANLEY MYERS

When I go to a show where the set is used only as a background to the proceedings I feel uneasy, although this particular bugbear may have been a help to me when, as a young dancer, I was called on to stage numbers and sketches for revue. Making use of the whole picture can add a visual life to what you are doing. However, being able to stage numbers successfully is a far cry from directing a whole show. That would be a GIANT leap – even to consider – not only in terms of the enormous responsibility involved, but in understanding, *and* acquiring the knowledge and support that the writers, actors and producers demand of their director. That I dared to take this leap is due entirely to the pushing and goading of one man – my husband – the composer Stanley Myers. Without doubt I owe him my career.

I was a dancer when we first met, doing reasonably well, and perfectly content to remain a small fish in a big pond. This rather irritated Stanley. He genuinely couldn't understand anyone who didn't wish to better themselves – and the lives of those around them while they were at it. Otherwise, as he would say, what's the point?

This was a wake-up call as far as I was concerned; I knew he was right, and I started to take jobs I never would have dreamed of taking without his being there. Stanley was the wind in my sails. He kept me on my toes. Right to the end, though our marriage hadn't lasted, he would come round to my place and at a certain point wander off from room to room. I never asked him what he was up to. I knew. He was checking to see if there were any tell-tale signs of my standards having slipped. He would hate that. To be honest, Stanley wasn't husband material – any more than I knew what it meant to be even a half-good wife; but we'd been through the mill together – a bond nothing and no one could alter. Once he had made the grade, I think Stanley would have liked to have seen me in a meadow like a race-horse put out to grass, gazing peacefully over many fences …

When Stanley died, the film director Nicolas Roeg wrote, "I am certain that Stanley's gift to the world of musical composition and communication will be appreciated more and more with the passing years. He will not be forgotten, his music is all around us. His wit, charm and eloquence will be sadly missed." Graham Preskett wrote: "Stanley's enemies were cant, dishonesty, sentimentality and moralisation. His friends: conviviality and a job well done."

Not long ago, some eighteen years after he had died, the radio programme *Classic FM* referred to Stanley as "the legendary Stanley Myers." How I wished he could have been there to hear it, for no one, absolutely no one I have ever known, suffered as Stanley did when he wasn't working. He would descend into a black hole of depression, seldom going out, except to the betting shop, silently playing patience for days on end. It was painful to be around him because the depression didn't seem like the usual sense of rejection we all feel when out of work, but more like a real conviction that it would always be like this and that somehow it was deserved. Now with hindsight, an exact science so they say, I believe this came from his feelings about his Jewish heritage. It was as if he saw himself as he thought others saw him: not really quite one of us.

In the notes Stanley wrote for our son Nicolas shortly before he died, he gives his reasons:

> *I never denied being a Jew, or wished not to be a Jew, but there were many aspects of Judaism as practised by my parents that nauseated me. My parents were three-times-a-year Jews – Passover, New Year and The Day of Atonement. But the majority of their friends were Jewish and I resented the way they talked about "goys" and "Shiksas." After all my nanny was both.*

Stanley was born and brought up in Birmingham. His father Maurice Myers, the eldest son of a tailor called Isaac Zellermyer, was the Birmingham representative for British Lion films, a company that made B feature films for the British Quota. Stanley's mother Ida Berker owned a very successful dress shop next to Birmingham's Theatre Royal. She dressed many of the local dignitaries. These included the Lady Mayoress, the actress Margaret Leighton and the beautiful musical star Dorothy Ward whose husband Shaun Glenville shared a liking for whiskey with Stanley's father. In 1942 Maurice Myers lost his job with British Lion and as Stanley wrote, "For the rest of his life he had time on his hands."

Ida kept the family and was seldom at home. Maurice took to drinking too much and scouring the countryside for black-market food which he would lay like trophies at Ida's feet in justification for his spent days. Ida was not impressed.

> *My father's temper had always been violent and I was one of the main target areas. But now there was almost no relief. When I got back from school there was the black car in the drive. The routine never varied. He would return from drinking around 3 o'clock, slam a few doors and go to bed. After an hour or two he would come downstairs with nothing to do but vent his rage. However I had an escape-route. A few hundred yards up the road was the house of Peter Smart, whose mother was sluttish and amiable and*

whose father was pipe-smoking and taciturn. I don't think they ever shouted at each other. I felt it was to do with being Christian and normal instead of Jewish and crazy. Of course I could never invite Peter to my house, or anybody else. I would have been ashamed for them to know what went on.

But... there was something far more important in Stanley's life, something that would free him and remain with him for ever. In his notes he puts it this way:

I was given one supreme gift: the love of music. From the earliest age that I can remember, I loved listening to records and the radio – the pop music of the '30s and '40s. Somehow it had a strange effect on me – I could taste the tunes, they were as vivid to me as food or smells. On my ninth birthday Anna Senz, the beautiful Viennese nanny who shared my room and wore black underwear, gave me a twelve-inch record of Ravel's Bolero and the whole world turned on its axis.

Almost solo, for his parents weren't very interested, Stanley started to educate himself musically. He bought records and went as often as he could to The City of Birmingham's Symphony Orchestra. He studied Donald Francis Tovey's *Essays on Musical Analysis* which led him to Sibelius:

Sibelius's fifth and seventh symphonies brought a new dimension to my life. Later I discovered that Sibelius was a very heavy drinker and from 1926 to his death in 1956 (aged eighty) he never published a note of significant music. It didn't matter. Two or three days ago I listened to the last movement of the fifth on the car radio – it just happened to be on. And it was hard not to weep. Not because of sadness, but through the sheer nobility of the human spirit that burns through the music.

He ends his notes touchingly, remembering a day spent with his father at the Cheltenham races. (Stanley's other passion was the horses).

Many exciting people were drinking champagne. I don't think my father said a cross word to me all day. He was charming. And when he was charming the birds would swoon in the trees and flutter to earth with a seraphic smile on their beaks. I forgot to mention he was nearly as good a dancer as Fred Astaire. Perhaps that's why my mother stayed with him.

Not long after that moment of listening in the car to Sibelius's fifth symphony Stanley died of cancer. He was 63. It was the 9th November. Kristallnacht 1993. There was no sound of broken glass that night as there had been on that date in 1938 when the Nazis smashed every shop window belonging to a Jew, but there were broken hearts. Many broken hearts. My own in particular.

La Vie Bohème

Stanley and 1 met in February 1954. One could say it was a bumpy first encounter. I was working in a revue at the little New Lindsay Theatre Notting Hill; one of four girls and four boys. Digby Wolfe, one of the actors, came into our dressing-room one night to tell us that he and his friend Stanley Myers were performing their cabaret act at Clement Freud's club above the Royal Court Theatre the following night and we were all invited. We dressed in our best for this late night outing, and Stanley Myers picked us up in his car after our show at 10.30 p.m. Digby sat in the back with Joan Sims and Dilys Laye and I sat in front with this glamorous stranger. It was glamorous to have a car at his age. Within seconds Stanley had crashed the car and I was thrown through the windscreen. After having four stitches in my head I arrived too late for the cabaret. The next day there was a huge bunch of flowers left for me at the stage door – another rather glamorous grown-up gesture; none of us had any money. There was a note:

> *Only you could make a crepe bandage look like*
> *a chic hat from Paris. Forgive me, Stanley Myers.*

I rather hoped he would come round, but he didn't. That was not his way: –

> *I was an outsider* [he wrote]. *This began*
> *when I moved from preparatory school to King*

Edward VI High School for Boys There were some 600 pupils and I was one of a dozen or so Jews. School began with prayers and announcements. We waited outside while Christ was invoked, then after 588 voices were raised in hymn, we were allowed in. A long wait for a small band of infidels. The war took my outsider image to bizarre lengths. I secretly welcomed German successes. And this feeling of being the traitor/betrayer has stayed with me. I'm still (secretly) glad when England is beaten at cricket or football. In all my film-related fantasies I was the outsider. The strong, silent, infinitely myste- rious man from nowhere. Sergio Leone [director of the movie *The Good, the Bad, and the Ugly,* which starred Clint Eastwood as the loner] *got it exactly right in the mid-sixties.*

My revue moved successfully to the Criterion Theatre as *Intimacy at 8.30,* and later that year I began rehearsing a cabaret show for Churchill's night club. The extra eleven pounds a week on top of the £20 a week I was earning at the Criterion was a help. It was perhaps auspicious that my solo, choreographed by Michael Charnley was to the song *Let There Be Love,* because when it came to the band call, there playing the piano in Barry Morgan's Band was the man from nowhere Stanley Myers. And that was it – I very quickly fell in love with him. Very much in love. He was a Prince to me with something sad behind hazel eyes. A Knight in shining armour. I never thought anyone would actually want to be with me; I was still a creature of my generation: brought up to be seen and not heard, *and* I wore glasses and never thought of myself as pretty. Also having left school at fifteen to train as a dancer I was no match for this highly educated man who had won a scholarship to Balliol and the Gold Medal at the Trinity School of Music. I felt I was the luckiest girl in the world. My euphoria was dashed somewhat when Stanley took me to Birmingham to meet his parents. His mother refused to address a single word to me.

"Does she eat potatoes?" she asked Stanley.

"I don't know," he replied. "Why don't you ask her?" But she couldn't. She couldn't stand the prospect of a Shiksa in the family.

They wrote to Stanley: "If you need help in getting rid of this girl..." I was aware of the horrors of anti-semitism, but now it seemed I was copping it myself, only the other way around. However, Stanley refused to take any of it seriously and laughed his way through.

We laughed a lot in those early years. I was still in the show at the Criterion and Stanley was picking up what jobs he could as a musician, mostly as a pianist in a band or as an accompanist to a cabaret artist. He very much needed to prove himself, and once said to me "You don't understand what it is to be Jewish – you not only have to do better this year than the last, you have to be seen to be doing better." He kept at it and although no job was too humble or too small for him, he still retained that endearing gift of the admiration for others. Hear him describe Jack Benny's performance at the Palladium or

Ella Fitzgerald in concert and you would be blown away by his sheer delight in their genius. He had a sneaking admiration for the bad guys too: the punters, the bookies and even the odd crook. There were plenty of those around in the 50s, men who made money on the black market during the war and were now going into business.

One of these was Maurie Connoly, whom we met one night at Harry Green's club in Soho. He asked if Stanley and I would be interested in producing the cabaret for his new club in Jermyn Street. We certainly were, and felt even better when on arrival we were offered a meal on the house. Veal escalope with tinned cherries, I remember, which we thoroughly enjoyed before being ushered into Maurie's private and rather plush office. Maurie indicated the two chairs at his desk where we sat patiently while Maurie lit a cigar.

"Now I want this show to 'ave, you know, a lo' of class," he said. Suddenly, the door burst open and a man with a knife threw himself across the desk and grabbed Maurie by the throat. Stanley and I were flattened against the walls on either side. "I'll get you for this, you little fucker," he shouted. "Fucking bastard, you'll never..."

Within seconds (it seemed like hours) two henchmen rushed in, grabbed the intruder and heaved him out of the room slamming the door behind them. In the silence that followed we stared at Maurie while he re-lit his cigar with a distinctly shaking hand.

"Oo was 'e?" he eventually blurted out. "I never seen the geezer before – 'ave you?"

I was pretty shaken, and glad to get out alive, but Stanley was fascinated by it all. "He must have had a bell under his desk. I saw his legs working overtime. And how about that face of innocence when he said 'Oo was 'e?' – as if *we* should know!!"

Where Stanley led, I followed – a bit like a docile rabbit. He was a Socialist, I became Socialist. He loved Jewish jokes – I loved Jewish jokes, and our great treat was to go round to Miriam Karlin's place where she and her friend Arnold had an endless supply. Stanley was used to kosher food, and I became used to kosher food. Should we meet before the show it would be at the Nosh Bar in Windmill Street. Stanley would order a salt beef sandwich and I matzos and chopped liver, proudly remembering to add, "Without the shmaltz, please."

I even took up Jewish instruction, and rather regret that neither of us took it too seriously. It annoyed Stanley to think I had been forced into it. To get around the problem of my not being Jewish we married in secret on 29th July 1955 renting a small bed-sit in Knightsbridge with shared bathroom and kitchen. Quite simply I adored Stanley, but I think I knew he didn't feel the same. He gave me something different, something in many ways far better: he made me feel I mattered. Whatever I did, good, bad or indifferent, it mattered. And to be honest this never changed. However far apart we became I always knew I, and whatever I was up to, mattered to him. It kept me on my toes hoping – and not always succeeding – to please him.

We were a 50s couple. We hadn't much money, but nor had most people of our age, so it didn't matter. We laughed our heads off at Tony Hancock on the radio and at the records of Tom Lehrer, Elaine May and Mike Nichols. If we had managed to get hold of an LP record of an American musical, we'd invite friends round and over a bottle of chianti listen to it in awe and reverence. Stanley knew the head waiter at the Café de Paris, so although we weren't allowed down the famous staircase to dance with the rich and famous, he'd manage to sneak us onto the balcony where we watched wonderful people like Marlene Dietrich, Noël Coward, and Pearl Bailey. Stanley wrote me a song which Adele Leigh recorded in the 60s:

When we first got married
We hadn't much money
And it still hasn't come our way
But we join the ranks
Of the rich and the leisured
Every seventh day...

We live the simple life
No expensive things for us
Our flat has just one room
Two rooms are too much fuss
But we're content you see
We have our luxury –
We get up late on Sundays...

We're very ordinary

We don't even own a car
That doesn't worry us
We like things as they are
Heaven's not far to seek
It comes around each week
We get up late on Sundays...

Some girls I know have diamonds and mink
They think its lots of fun
But when I come to work it out
I think that I'm the lucky one –

Some people fly to Rome
For a change of atmosphere
We holiday at home
Fifty-two times a year
It's much more fun we find
To leave the world behind
And get up late on Sundays
So very late on Sundays...

But I had to be careful never to overstep the mark: never to become a burden. I once took Stanley's arm on Shaftesbury Avenue and he turned on me and shook me off. "Don't ever lean on me emotionally – do you understand?" The vehemence of this outburst shook me. And again after we'd been to see Bartok's *Bluebeard's Castle* he was at pains to explain to me that each and every man needed a private place to which no one should have a key. I thought of Bluebeard's strung-up wives and took the point! Had I been older I would have known that Stanley's need for his own space and solitude was the composer in him.

Things changed when I became pregnant. I didn't know how Stanley would take the news, but he actually jumped for joy and did what he called his Serge Lifar leaps all down Lower Regent Street and back while I stood on the corner of Piccadilly Circus laughing till I cried. He might have looked like Serge Lifar but he was no dancer.

Stanley's first personal success came with his ballet music for the musical *A Girl Called Jo*. Suddenly Stanley was recognised as a composer of considerable talent. Somehow he could sense exactly what was needed musically and this discernment was to distinguish him from other composers in the years to come. The choreographer Michael Charnley became his fan for life. Unfortunately the joy of this moment, which had been some time coming, coincided with the imminent arrival of our son. It was too much for Stanley, and he became very ill. First jaundice and later a skin disease which landed him in hospital. The steroids they gave him made him swell up and it terrified him. I witnessed for the first time his descent into that black hole of despair. It was as if life had crushed him. He had missed his one chance, he would never be employed again; he probably wouldn't recover, how did I imagine we were going to live... And I, used to the stiff-upper-lip of my own family – a rather remote father and a stoical mother who would never complain about anything – found the intimacy of his torment both astonishing and quite shattering. I sat silently at his bedside unable to respond, but the anguish I felt for him altered the rest of my life. Before going home, in the hospital toilet and heavily pregnant, I got down on my knees and prayed to God to make me a stronger person. No more docile rabbit. I realized that Stanley was unable to cope with the thought of being a parent, and felt that it would be best all round if I took on that job by myself. Stanley's happiness was my happiness. He must be free to work, and I must take care of our baby.

Stanley, Fiz and Nic, 1956

Ah well, I was young. It took years of growing up for me to be able to confront one of his depressions and say, "Stanley, you may be having one of your attacks", and years more for Stanley to be able to smile back at me sheepishly and say "Maybe!" But I never doubted his pain.

Our son Nicolas was born two days after Stanley came out of hospital. We were living in Green Street, this time with our own bathroom but still just one room. Stanley arranged for us to move to a small flat in St John's Wood. He got a job writing with Peter Myers on his revue *For Amusement Only*. Sadly Peter already had his composers, but it kept Stanley very busy and with the odd gig here or there, I was much alone with my babe. We were very poor. What bits and pieces of jewellery I had from godparents or aunts and uncles all went to the pawn shop. Someone lent me an electric fire for Nic's room, someone else gave me a Horrocks housecoat – pink and white spots, I remember. Stanley came home and said, "What have you got on? You're not middle-aged for heavens' sake!"

I was finding it hard to make Stanley happy. I soon discovered he was having an affair with the dancer in the revue. One of those insensitive know-alls – an actress in the show – phoned to tell me that Stanley and the dancer had been in her dressing-room to say how concerned they were that their affair was causing me pain. "I thought you'd like to know that," she said. I put the phone down on her. I felt my whole world had come to an end. That night I screwed up the courage to ask Stanley, "Does this mean divorce?" He seemed faintly surprised. "I shouldn't think so," he said, and turned over. I would wake banging my head against the bed head. I was feeling abandoned.

What helped, funnily enough, was Stanley having one of his attacks. This time screaming failure. He was a failure, I was a failure, he had married a dancer not a housewife, we were going nowhere. As usual I said nothing, but oh boy did I decide to get back to work. And as soon as possible. First I agreed to choreograph a Summer Season in Weymouth – which in those days meant three shows. Monkey, my dancer friend (the very talented Diana Monks), took care of Nicolas for me. The show was a lot of work, but it led to my being called to choreograph, and then to direct, the musical *Grab Me a Gondola* at the Theatre Royal Windsor, with Stanley as musical director. The show was an instant hit, and Donald Albery brought it to the West End.

Stanley and I were back on track. We could afford some help at home – Luisa Puente Alba, the Spanish mother's help, became our life-long friend – and Stanley was happy – well, almost. In truth he longed to be composing his own music, so the job of musical director was not entirely satisfactory. He disliked rehearsals, and the endless repetition to get it right; but most of all he loathed the obligatory buttering up of egos. He would distance himself by having a copy of *The Sporting Life* on his knees while he sat at the piano. But he was always professional, and I used to marvel at the way he was always spot on when called to play, proving he had kept one ear alert to the proceedings.

As soon as rehearsals were over Stanley and a writer named Alec Graham started work on a musical based on the life of Nell Gwynne to be called *Pretty Witty Nell*. I mentioned this one day to Donald Albery and he asked to see it. To our great joy Donald bought an option and approached Joan Plowright to play Nell Gwynne. For Stanley to have his own musical in the West End was like a dream come true. No longer would his father be able to goad him with "Has Fiz found you another job, Stanley?" – just as years later Stanley was to goad our son: on hearing he was off to LA to run a music video company, "Oh yes," Stanley said, "and what are you going to do when you grow up?" These Jewish guys were tough on each other.

After watching the show one night, Ann Jenkins, Donald Albery's production assistant, hailed a cab and offered to give me a lift. On the way she told me that Joan Plowright, who was much in demand, had taken another job, and that as a result Donald had decided not to go ahead with *Pretty, Witty Nell*. Would I tell Stanley?

Had she hit me over the head with a sledge hammer it would have been less shattering. "But Stanley will be devastated," I said. I can still see her nasty, smiling face lit up by the street lamps at the back of that taxi. She was a cruel woman and well known for it. "I'm sure he'll get over it," was all she said. Had they no idea of the work and the talent Stanley had invested in that show? Of course they had.

"No he won't," I said, and I cried outside our flat trying to gather the courage to go in and break the news. It was Donald Albery who should have done the job himself; my having to tell Stanley would add insult to injury.

Again it was as if life had crushed him and the deep black pit engulfed him. I'd go to work (by now working on a revue for Michael Codron), and return to find him on the sofa in exactly the same position, as if he hadn't moved. I longed to help him, but I couldn't. I felt the pain, but lacked the knowledge and understanding to deal with it. We never talked about this to anyone. Our neighbour Sandy Wilson was very helpful at this time. He was the writer and composer of London's big success *The Boy Friend* and he was an admirer of Stanley's talent. He would ask us over to his very pretty house in Hampstead, and he bought me a 'Sack' dress, a sort of 50's version of a 20s style, and I was thrilled.

At the beginning of 1958 I was written up as "the young director with three shows running in the West End." Stanley was still struggling. But he arranged a move, this time a seven year lease on a flat in Eaton Place. He always made all the arrangements and even chose the flat himself. He was very good at that sort of thing, each time finding something a little better. There was a moment of hope when the producer Harry Saltzman asked to see Stanley. I went with him and there in a dark corner sat the very famous John Osborne. He handed Stanley the script of his new musical *Paul Slickey*, saying nonchalantly, "See how you get on with it". We skipped all the way back down Eaton Square, but Stanley had only written two songs before he was told that Jock Addison had been hired as composer. This was less of a blow than it might have been, as the show turned out to be a resounding flop.

In 1959 Stanley and I worked on a revue together called *One to Another*. Stanley was its musical director. He composed the music for sketches by Dorothy Parker, Robert Benchley and John Mortimer. As usual he distanced himself during rehearsals by burying himself in a mass of newspapers – never, though, missing a cue. Actually he was distancing himself in more ways than one. To prepare for an audition he had been rehearsing an actress at home for the Nell Gwynne part. He and Alec still wanted to see *Pretty, Witty Nell* in production, as it deserved to be.

One evening I got home to find Stanley with a suitcase. He had decided to go and live with the actress, and so he went. Nic and I tried to hold onto him at the door, but he left … As in the Judy Garland song:

The road gets rougher,
It's lonelier and tougher.
That great beginning
Has seen its final inning
And all because of
The Man that got away …

I had to keep working, but at night I would sit in the bay window listening to the London traffic. I knew the sound of Stanley's car. I lost a stone in weight.

I did flounder, and badly, but I was held together by three things: first, our son – I had to be okay for him; second, by the enormous amount of work I had on hand; and lastly because, deep down, I felt Stanley would come home... one day.

Two months later I had a letter from Stanley telling me that he was now living alone, which he said had been thrust on him by shortage of money.

> *But now that it has happened [he wrote] I should like to stick to it at least for the time being. Not that I don't get pangs. I felt for some obscure reason very jealous that you were going out with Lindsay Anderson the other night and had to go out myself to calm down. It has come to me very forcibly that for various reasons I created an image to myself of what I wanted you to be and this image has boomeranged on me. I mean of course the glamour of having a very important wife. Well, you became one and that led to a lot of other things. What I'd left out of the account was this, and I can't explain it better than by quoting from a book (incidentally the marriage he describes was a failure, but isn't that life?) "Thus our whole life was given happiness by delight in certain aspects of one another. Sometimes when I came home, I paused in front of our house in the evening, and the feeling that she was in the flat upstairs was one of intoxicating wonder." When I read that, I thought how I too had felt the same about you, but more and more as time went on I had become concerned with whether Julian More or Joan Heal was up there, or whether Michael Codron or Donald Albery had telephoned and all the rest of it. Well,*

quite often they were and that was splendid, and you were important and sought after. And that became much more important to me than just you, the girl I had married. And anyway we were both so busy that we never had the time or by then the wish to get back to those other things. It seems to me that I – we perhaps – but I started it, made the wrong choice.

I'd like you to give up work in some ways, though as things are and will be for some time, I couldn't keep you and Nic in moderate comfort on what I earn.

He went on to say that if we got together again we'd both have to work a lot harder and that he was prepared to do that with my help. He ended,

I feel towards you about the same as I did when you lived in the Ranee's flat.

And this was my beautiful husband about whom I still felt the same as I had done when he lived round the corner in Albion Street. But he was right. It was because of the enormous pressure of my work that I had left him too much alone. All I wanted now was for him to come home so that I could put that right. He did come home – but a year and a half later, clearly with no idea how much that year and a half alone had hurt me. He simply picked up where he had left off; not because he was callous – far from it – but because he didn't empathise.

Nor did it occur to him that I might have had suitors. Being alone I had quite a few, among them the warm-hearted handsome actor Nigel Davenport whom I was to lead a terrible dance. But Stanley knew me too well: he knew he came first.

Through my work at the Royal Court Stanley met and got on well with the poet Christopher Logue. Together they wrote songs for Peter Cook's *Establishment Club* which was where things were happening in the early 60s. His best friend from his Balliol days – the very talented Canadian film director Paul Almond – came over to do some TV films, *and* he wanted Stanley to do the music. Things were looking up. Later Stanley went over to Canada to work on one of Paul's movies – a *big* step for him. He wrote to me from there:

> *I was just thinking I wish I hadn't gone off with [the first girl] when we first got married. I'm sorry I did. I don't know how you have remained so loyal for so long because you're not a fool, but thank you. I only seem to be able to think straight (or at all) when I'm on my own.* (Letter of August 27 1963.)

And there it was again: "on my own." I kept on working, also on my own!

After *Beyond the Fringe* I went almost straight on to co-directing the musical *Blitz* with Lionel Bart, during which Stanley arranged another move – this time to Holland Park. We then worked together on a show starring Annie Ross, who became a great friend. On the surface things were trundling along quite smoothly, and Stanley was gaining ground; but in truth I was beginning to crash.

Nic was by now eight years old, and my faith in the Fairy Books to which I had clung – particularly the one that went "You must keep going until Stanley becomes recognised and then he will take over and we'll all live happily ever after" – was beginning to falter.

During my work on *Blitz* Stanley had had a woman to help him with the move to Holland Park. She happened to be a friend of Christopher Logue's. In an unguarded moment he mentioned casually that she might be having an affair with Stanley, adding admiringly, "You handle Stanley's affairs so well." He had assumed I knew all about it. I didn't, and I wasn't that admirable. I hit back by telephoning Nigel Davenport and arranging to meet up with him.

Our lives became a mess.

To try to improve things Stanley arranged for me and Nic to join him for a holiday in France, just the three of us together. We'd no sooner got there than Donald Albery telephoned asking me to return at once, as a principal in *Blitz* had to be replaced. Stanley told me to ring back and refuse to go. But I couldn't. It was a very bad decision vis à vis our marriage – perhaps the worst I ever made.

I didn't know at the time that it was Stanley's parents who had paid for our trip to France, hoping that it would keep us together; but my putting work first had proved to them that I didn't want that. I *did* want that. But the show must go on; and Donald Albery had been very good to me. I decided to go. This hurt Stanley, and at the same time provided him with the license to follow his own star. I remember my frustration at that time, feeling I was no longer able to please anyone – least of all myself. And especially not Stanley.

A new girl appeared on the scene – this time a psychiatrist; and I pushed off.

I took Nic and the nanny with me to live with Nigel Davenport, but I missed Stanley the whole time and was haunted by the thought that he had tried to keep us together – possibly more than I had. I put Nic and the nanny in a seaside hotel with his young cousin, and left for Rotterdam to direct a touring version of Lionel Bart's *Oliver*. I wrote to Stanley asking if we could come back home and he replied,

> *Dearest Horses [for Stanley "horses" was a real term of endearment!] My concern is this: – I'm telling the absolute truth as I know it because there can be no covering up or things left unsaid. You (and secondarily, Nic) mean more to me than anyone else has, does, or will – I feel differently about you to the way I feel about anyone else. My greatest ambition is to live happily with you for the rest of – whatever. On the other hand I can't disguise the fact that in some ways I am freer and easier when I'm on my own.*

One would think I should have got the message by now, but it was always couched in such gentle tones.

I feel a lot of money would help a great deal. In a way I don't think I ever got over the Pretty Witty Nell *business, and if the Fenella show comes off, or* The Scientists *was on I'd feel back on track again (Incidentally Frank Norman sent me a script of – yes, you've guessed it* A Café Up West.*) Joan Littlewood has suggested I do a new score though whether anything comes of it I've no idea. Whatever happens the flat will be ready and paid for the moment you return. It would be lovely to talk things over with you among the tulip-fields, drinking champagne or whatever you do in Holland.*

But he never came. I waited long months and eventually went to Marriage Guidance. I can remember sitting opposite this tweed-suited woman arrogantly thinking – what could she possibly know about lives like ours; but she listened patiently as I blurted out my tales of woe, put down her pen and said, "Do you want to be married to someone who doesn't want to be married?" I stared back. It was as though someone had lifted a big black cloud of denial from my shoulders. Of course, at last I understood that Stanley must be free to be happy.

The next day I started divorce proceedings. Apart from my son, I closed the door on the world. And a few weeks later my doctor, alerted by friends, sent me to a psychotherapist: the eminent Dr Graham-Howe of Queen Anne Street.

"And what brings you here?" he asked.

"Self-destruction," I replied, trying to sound *au fait* with the jargon!

"Really, and what is that?"

Doesn't he know, I thought. "Well, I just sit at home, I never go out. I never answer the telephone – and as my son and I depend on my working for our livelihood it's not very sensible."

At the end of that first session Dr Graham-Howe called me back at the door. "Oh, by the way," he said, "not self-destruction, self-preservation."

He was very brilliant at his work, quite hard, and always straight to the point. For instance when I told him about Stanley's attacks of torment, and how they would suddenly stop the moment I broke down myself, the doctor said calmly, "Well, of course. You'd proved he existed." Wow! When I hit the street later I ran from call-box to call-box trying to find one that wasn't bust, just to be able to hear Stanley's voice. When I did finally get through, he was working and sounded irritated by my call. I was relieved... sort of.

Dr Graham-Howe didn't keep me long; he didn't believe in lengthy treatment. Before leaving I said, "It seems to me I loved Stanley with all my heart – but look what happened. Maybe I don't know what love is."

"Do you want to know?" he said.

"Yes," I said. He took a card form his desk drawer and wrote: "Q. What is love? A. Love is what sets the other free."

I still have that card. "Thank you" I said.

Stanley *was* happier. It wasn't long before he found his own métier, which was writing music for film or TV. No more actors' egos or endless repetitive rehearsals. He could sit at his own piano, plug in the movieola, and (on the whole) work the hours he chose. The only people he had to deal with were the producers and directors. Nicholas Roeg and Volka Schlendorf, Stephen Frears and Norma Heyman were four he was particularly fond of. The scores he wrote for the directors Jack Smight (*Kaleidoscope* and *Ulysses*) and Michael Cimino *(The Deer Hunter)* won him several Golden Discs, various awards, and a great deal of money. He remained a musicians' musician who liked to play the horses; for a while he shared a race-horse with Albert Finney. Stanley was never short of beautiful women to look after him, one of whom he married, and the last of whom was younger than our son. I think they all knew his music came first.

In *Modern Man in Search of a Soul* the profound Dr Carl Jung explains it all thus:

The artist's life cannot be otherwise than full of conflicts, for two forces are at war in him: on the one hand a common longing for happiness, satisfaction and security and on the other a ruthless passion for creation which may go so far as to override every personal desire.

When Stanley was diagnosed with cancer in August 1993 – and he had it everywhere – he typically went into denial mode. He left all medical discussions and decisions to our son Nicolas, with the one oft-repeated proviso, "My agent mustn't know anything about this." Brigitte,

Stanley's second wife, returned from Spain to nurse him and we were all sworn to secrecy. All Stanley's remaining energy went into the TV series *Middlemarch*.

Stanley Myers, 1993

Somehow its director, Anthony Page, got wind of Stanley's illness. "Is this true?" he asked me, clearly concerned for his production.

Anthony is a great friend and one I would never lie to in normal circumstances, but I looked him straight in the face and said, "I don't know what this is all about, Anthony. I have this minute been talking to Stanley and he is very pleased with what he's writing for you. It's unusual for Stanley to say this. I think you're going to get the score of a lifetime."

A month or so later Anthony telephoned to say, "You were right, Fiz. We did get the score of a lifetime!" He arranged for the recordings to be played back to Stanley at the hospital so he could discuss the mixing. Nicolas arranged a BBC recording of Stanley's *Concerto for Soprano Saxaphone*. They pulled the plug on the life support as it came over the air, and Stanley slipped away listening to his concerto. At the funeral John Williams played Stanley's beautiful *Cavatina*.

There is a tradition at the Liberal Jewish Synagogue for a person's name to be read out on the anniversary of their death. A year after Stanley's death my dear friend Linda Drew took me there to arrange this for Stanley.

I signed on for a course on Judaism; partly unfinished business and partly because I was still searching... for Stanley, I suppose. I did find quite a lot of him – for example in their understanding of man's duality of nature: the good side, and the evil side which can be used creatively as long as that creativity never becomes selfish, greedy or grabbing. This can only be avoided by hard work and good deeds. Above all one must strive to make the world a better place for present and future generations. I recognized aspects of Stanley's morality in all of this; but of course I was never going to find him, the self-styled "man from nowhere" – he wouldn't want it. His legacy lies in his offspring and his music and that's how he'd want it to be. It's just that I wanted to show how much it had taken him to get there. Something of what it actually took. His life for a start.

13

NOT SO ANGRY AFTER ALL:
JOHN OSBORNE

Of all creative artists I have ever worked with the best known, and most talked about and read about, was John Osborne. There was a time, after his play *Look Back in Anger* had opened at the Royal Court in 1956, when it was almost impossible to pick up a newspaper without there being an article, profile, photograph or quote on John Osborne, the media's first "Angry Young Man." He was a Star; young, elegant, and talented, with a unique mastery of the English Language which he could use to devastating effect.

Not Oxbridge, but from a red-brick university, Osborne seemed to speak for our generation. I can remember the thrill when Stanley managed to get seats for the

midnight matinée of *The Entertainer*, and we glimpsed
John Osborne and his wife Mary Ure standing outside the
theatre in their evening clothes. They seemed so glamorous; part of another world. The star-studded world of the
rich and famous.

Years later, in 1965, I was to work for the awesome
Angry Young Man, and I found him to be retiring and
painfully vulnerable.

Anthony Page cast me as Liz in Osborne's play
Inadmissible Evidence, starring Nicol Williamson and
John Hurt. We opened in Brighton and Osborne gave us
all printed copies of the play as an opening night present.
In mine he has written: "Dear Fiz, with gratitude and
admiration, Love, John."

This was beyond belief kind, because in fact I was
rubbish. I was no actress. Just how to play an intimate scene
and be heard at the back of the gallery was beyond me.
The front of house manager came round to my dressing
room to tell me there had been many complaints about
my inaudibility. In London the kinder critics ignored me,
although I do remember reading one review that said
something like "there is one performance that has to be
the worst seen on any stage ever" – or words to that effect.
I had to put the paper down, walk slowly downstairs and
wait in the wings to go on and repeat the outrage. It was
tough. My marriage had failed and I – who had taken the
job as the kind of challenge that might raise the spirits –
was failing again.

I can remember telling Ann Beach, the actress with
whom I was sharing a dressing room, that I felt like a

walking tank full of tears, and I was afraid someone might push me, for then I'd fall and spill over ... Ann listened patiently without comment. I wasn't often a drama queen!

However, during the run John asked me if I would assist him on the play *Meals on Wheels*, which he was about to direct for the Royal Court Theatre. This too turned out to be a tricky assignment, for John's idea of directing seemed to be turning the pages of the script and laughing while the actors floundered about. It was if he thought the writing was all, and the production would somehow leap off the page. It doesn't!

None of us knew what he was after, and this made him difficult to assist. We struggled our way through, which John seemed to accept as fine. It wasn't! For some time after the show had quietly opened and closed, the brilliant Roy Kinnear (fortunately for the show, one of the actors), would come bounding over to me and say,

"Remember *Meals on Wheels*?"

"Not much," I'd reply.

"*Exactly!*" he'd say – and double over with laughter.

But during those rather agonizing rehearsals of *Meals*, and the on-going run of *Inadmissible*, John asked me one day in a coffee break if I'd seen that day's newspaper. I knew the critics had been to *Inadmissible* the night before, as Alan Dobie had taken over the lead from Nicol Williamson, who was leaving for the New York production.

"No, John, I haven't," I said. "I haven't dared."

John put down his coffee and *ran*. I watched him running down the street towards his house in Chester Square, returning with the *Financial Times*, which, amazingly, had singled me out for special mention. It was very sweet of him. I realized that without ever saying a word he must have known what I'd been though.

"We'll have a glass of champagne later," he said.

And there was another moment when John arrived at rehearsal visibly shaken.

"I've just passed a woman sobbing in the street – sobbing out loud." He was hardly able to get the words out.

Yet this hugely empathetic and vulnerable man could lash out in print like no other. He railed against the world: his mother, his wives, England, and particularly any form of change. For example, he hit out against any revised version of the King James Bible and the loss of its beautiful Jacobean English. He raged against what he saw as the technological take-over, with its (and I quote) "terrifying need for a forward-looking, outward-looking programme-controlled machine-tool reassessment. With yes, facilities of memory and judgement far beyond the capacity of any human grief – being. Or any human being that has ever lived."

In a way one might call John a stick-in-the-mud, or a sentimental old fool – indeed, I have heard it said that the underlying sentimentality in all his work stopped him from progressing as perhaps he might have. To me it was anguish, and from the little I know of him I feel I can vouch for the fact that the anguish underlying so many of his outbursts was genuine. And painful.

"I prefer the upper classes, don't you?" John asked me one evening at the Royal Court Hotel. We were waiting for his play *A Sense of Detachment*, on which I had done some work, to open at the Court.

"Well, except for their cruelty," I replied rather flippantly. John's reaction was astonishing. He put down his glass, went white as a sheet, and stared at me as if I had made some earth-shattering remark. Luckily his fourth wife Jill Bennett arrived and the moment passed.

A Sense of Detachment is of course an ironic title. There was nothing detached about John, and there never would be. John came out of his corner boxing ...

He had been brought up in Devon where his mother Nellie Beatrice worked in a pub. Linda Drew, who was P.A. to him and Jill, thought there was much resentment there, although he was in fact very good to his mother. Less so to his ex-wives, who came in for much unkind and undeserved vitriol. As later did many of his colleagues. John Osborne's brilliance had turned mean-spirited.

When he slandered Jill Bennett in his autobiography, dumping her for his fifth wife Helen Dawson, a very intelligent journalist, Jill's friends, myself included, went off John. We did not buy his books or go to his plays. It would not have mattered to John; he had moved on. It seemed he had at last got what he wanted: life as a country gent; a large house hidden away in the Hereford countryside, and a wife who adored him. By all accounts they happily knocked back the booze together with impunity. One might think that all this, to quote John, had "fugitive reasons," but evidently not, for they invited a TV company to make a documentary about their life. Helen was seen picking roses with the gardener and bringing in the garden produce, while John sat poring over a pile of scrap-books filled with cuttings of his past glories.

Barry Humphries, who also saw the programme, thought Osborne "looked like a cosy old stage-doorman." He did, rather! A happy one, though — at long last ...

14

A BRIEF ENCOUNTER ON THE GENTLE SIDE:
BINKIE BEAUMONT

Hugh "Binkie" Beaumont was the managing director of H. M. Tennant Ltd, London's leading theatrical producers. Sheridan Morley called him "the most powerful theatrical producer in London from the 1940's to the mid-1960's." His typographic red, black and white posters were unmistakable. His stars included John Gielgud, Edith Evans and Peggy Ashcroft.

After my years with Donald Albery, I never expected to work for his rival; but I did, and in a way that took me completely by surprise.

It was 1969 when he phoned me.

"Miss Fazan, Binkie Beaumont here." The voice was quiet, careful and precise. I didn't recognise it because I'd never met him. Quite frankly, I thought someone was pulling my leg.

"Oh yes," I replied, waiting for whoever it was to reveal themselves. But it was indeed him. He told me that he was putting on a production of *A Flea in Her Ear* in which Elizabeth Seal was to star. Things hadn't been going well for her, he said, and both the director, Jaques Charon, and the adapter, John Mortimer, wanted her replaced.

"I should explain, Miss Fazan, that Miss Seal has done wonderful things for me in the past, and I owe her a great deal. It's simply that her recent private life has been extremely hard on her."

I wasn't used to this; I could hardly believe my ears. Could it be that here was a man who accepted that life had its blows, and yet did not run away or drop its victims like a hot brick? I almost blacked out.

"You see," he continued, as quietly and carefully as before, "I have no intention of doing the play without her."

He asked if I would accept an engagement as a personal coach to Liz Seal. It would involve attending rehearsals in Brighton and London and working privately with Liz whenever she was free. I accepted the job at once, and was to discover that Binkie Beaumont was not only stubborn, as all artists are, but loyal and civilised too. He also loved a good family gossip.

I spent many evenings with him at the Ship Hotel in Brighton after the show. It seemed a quiet gossip was Binkie Beaumont's form of escape. We talked of Liz and her turbulent relationship with her jealous and sadistic husband; of Maggie Leighton and her relationship with the younger Laurence Hervey; of my own life.

The show, a French farce, went reasonably well, though I never felt it was as good as it could have been. All the same, Liz Seal and Binkie Beaumont saw it honourably through to its end, without fear and without reproach. This was a man who cared.

15

LIFE ON THE HIGH WIRE: TONY RICHARDSON

I was buying tickets at the Royal Court Theatre in the early '60's, when I noticed a young man wandering around the foyer in a state of euphoria. "I can't believe I'm here," he said aloud. "I've dreamed about this in Australia, and now I'm actually standing in the foyer."

I smiled encouragingly. On these occasions one always prays that nothing will happen that might make the person change his mind. Such was the fame of the Royal Court, however, that the euphoria didn't surprise me at all.

Once a non-conformist chapel, the Royal Court had been a theatre since 1871, and in the early years of the twentieth century it had been the home of Bernard Shaw and Granville Barker. Its sudden and extraordinary rise in fame in the mid-'50's was due to its artistic director George Devine and his well-known belief in the right to fail. The Good Old Cause, one might call it today. It was George Devine's policy that the Royal Court should be a theatre that spoke for our time and that the plays performed there should be relevant to contemporary life. Novelists and playwrights were contracted from both sides of the Channel and this pioneering spirit influenced everyone who worked there.

George Devine, with his mass of white hair, tweeds and pipe, was a very approachable man. Sitting with him one day in the stalls of Wyndham's Theatre during the rehearsals for *Inadmissible Evidence*, in which I was playing a short part, I told him how odd I found it that having often worked into the small hours on the production side, I was much more exhausted by acting.

"I can understand that," he said. "That's why all actors drink." Rather surprised by this reply, I turned to him for an explanation, but George looked past me, got up hurriedly and moved quickly towards the exit. I wondered what it was that had made George jump. There in the doorway was the tall, thin figure of Tony Richardson, poised like Mercury himself. I understood at once. Tony was not one to be kept waiting.

Tony Richardson was born in Yorkshire in 1928. He told me that his days at school there were the most miserable of his life, and only when he got to Oxford University was he able to put all that behind him. He became the President of OUDS in 1949, started his career at BBC TV in 1952, and went on to direct at Stratford-on-Avon.

By 1955 he had met George Devine, made a strong impression, and become George's associate at the Royal Court. It was Tony's production of John Osborne's *Look Back in Anger* that changed the face of London's theatre. The labels "Angry Young Men" and "Kitchen Sink Drama" were coined then and there, and argued all over the Media. No one however could pin Tony down, he was such an independent spirit.

He and John Osborne started their own film company – Woodfall Films – beginning with the film versions of *Look Back in Anger* and *The Entertainer*, and going on to change the style of British cinema with their production of Karel Reisz's *Saturday Night and Sunday Morning* as well as Tony's own films – *The Loneliness of the Long Distance Runner*, *Taste of Honey* and *Tom Jones*, for which Tony won an Academy Award.

People would say that Tony could walk into a room, and by his very presence make things happen. I saw it, many a time. Taller than most, he moved fast. He would stride onto a film set in jeans and tennis shoes, followed by his entourage; his head turning from side to side and his hands waggling at the end of his long arms as though charged by a live wire. Surrounded by his assistants, he gave his orders quietly, in a faintly mocking way as if surprised these things hadn't already been done. He'd then retire, probably with friends for a glass of champagne, until they had. The good life was very important. Tony was generous and fun to work with and be with, but unnerving too. He was never, ever predictable.

In the mid-'70's he suddenly closed down the Woodfall office in Curzon Street and went to live in America. England was over – he'd had enough – and his intuitive sense of where things were happening made the leap to LA an easy one. Maybe it was revenge. Who knows? Certainly what he had achieved in twenty years was remarkable for the extent of the change he brought to theatre and film. He had never really received the recognition he deserved. He was more imitated than thanked or praised. And though he seemed to shrug off his critics in his devil-may-care way, something rankled, and he left England for good.

I first met Tony in 1961. He had sent me the script of a revue which he thought might suit the Royal Court and wondered if I'd be interested in directing it. I was touring in Brighton at the time, directing *Bonne Soupe* for Donald Albery. However, telegrams arrived, then messengers with scripts, and eventually, when I'd got back to London, a chauffeur-driven car came to take me to lunch. We drove to the Chiswick Mall, where Tony had rented the flat belonging to George Devine and his wife Sophie of the Motley sisters (distinguished designers of long standing). In some trepidation at meeting the dynamic Tony Richardson for the first time, I rang the doorbell. The place was light and bright with white-painted walls and arches leading to different floor levels tiled in chequered gray and white. Tony sat on the long plain sofa in jeans and white tennis shoes with one leg tucked up – like a sprinter waiting for the off. It took some courage to tell him that I didn't think the revue he had sent me was up to much. To my amazement, he dropped the whole idea immediately, and showed not the slightest dismay. Tony, I learned, was not one to persist; his time was too important.

He was friendly and curious – mostly about me, which I found rather unnerving. I knew I had been invited to discuss his revue because I had directed *Beyond the Fringe* – London's big hit of the moment. Actually he gave me the feeling that I was not at all what he had expected and that he found this quite fun. Again unnerving. (Could I keep this up? When can I go home?)

Tony Richardson directing "The Border".

Later that year Tony asked me to choreograph the dances for *The Changeling*, which he was to direct at the Royal Court. This Jacobean play by Thomas Middleton and William Rowley had not been performed professionally since the seventeenth century, and Tony, typically, was the first to resurrect it. He told me over the phone that the production was to be Goyaesque, and asked me to look up the Hora. I hadn't known Goya was Jewish, but never mind. I diligently looked up the Hora, even getting an Israeli dancer round who taught me a few Yemenite dances as well, just in case. Once into rehearsal, I soon realised it was the Spanish Jhota that Tony had been after. Not knowing it, I thought it best to Spanish up the Hora, hoping no one would notice. No one did! Fortunately for me, perhaps, something much more intriguing was going on. Mary Ure as Beatrice, and Robert Shaw as de Flores, met on this production and fell in love. Mary was still married to John Osborne at the time, and Tony saw himself as her protector. He was not averse to seeing Mary and John Osborne break up, but found Robert Shaw simply not good enough. Bob, on the other hand, told me that he longed to take Mary away from it all–there was something of the Knight in shining armour about Bob Shaw, and in time he and Mary were married.

Intrigue was the spice of life for Tony. It was surprising that someone as full of nervous energy should need that kind of stimulation, but he seemed to thrive on it in a humorous way, and people were drawn to him, knowing he was at the centre of what was going on. I learned to slip away. John Addison, the composer who worked on all of Tony's productions, noticed my absence. "Where do you get to?" he asked. "I often look around for you when we gather for drinks at the end of the day, but you're never there." He was right; I'd gone home. It was the only means I had of lasting the course.

There were several dances to choreograph on Tony's film of *Tom Jones*, and all involving dialogue; which was tricky. *Tom Jones* was a film that Tony had hawked round various British production companies for backing and none of them had wanted to know. In the end it was the American United Artists that put up the money for a low-budget movie, and Tony and the principal actors were forced to work for a share of the profits. As it turned out, it made them all millionaires.

During the shooting of the country dances for the Vauxhall scenes, which we shot at night in Holland Park, an unfortunate situation arose. The crowd dancers, whose union was FAA (the Film Artists' Association), found out that the Equity dancers were getting more money. They decided to strike, and at 3 a.m. shooting ground to a halt. Surrounded by the rebellious group, I was much relieved to see Tony stride over with his entourage, to help me – or so I thought. But all he said was: "I'm very surprised at you, Fiz. I thought you'd be able to handle this sort of thing. I mean, you don't expect us to sit around all night, do you? I mean – really!" And he strode off followed by the entourage; leaving me dumbfounded. It wasn't my business to sort out financial problems and the rebels knew it. It was all patched up quite quickly, and who knows how much that public rebuke did to help? Tony was very clever.

He was also very loyal, and though I never lost the feeling that at any moment I, or someone else, would be out on their ear, I continued to work with him; in all, four films and five shows. These were *Hamlet* in 1969, a big event which brought theatre to the Round House for the first time, and starred Nicol Williamson (who despite the success of the show was merciless in his imitations of Tony). Later, *The Threepenny Opera* and *Anthony and Cleopatra* with his ex-wife Vanessa Redgrave, and *I Claudius* in 1972, during the rehearsals of which we both watched the seventy-seven-year-old Robert Graves fall headlong from the high set of stairs into the orchestra pit. The distinguished old man had just been warning us that *I Claudius* had always had a jinx on it, and we both turned white thinking this was it – Robert Graves himself had copped it – he was dead. But no, he crawled out, and was fine. We laughed about it later. It was the production, I'm afraid, that was the disaster.

Then I worked with him on the films *Red and Blue*, which starred Vanessa again, though it had been designed for Jeanne Moreau; *The Charge of the Light Brigade* – again Vanessa, but this time Tony was recovering from an affair with Jeanne Moreau and the press were hounding him. In their enthusiasm for a story, they mistook me for her; and that caused a kerfuffle. Perhaps to put me in my place, Tony said one day, "I think I'll put you in the next scene, Fiz." He liked doing this. "Oh, Tony, please don't!" I said; but there was no arguing with Tony. "Stephen, find Fiz a costume." Stephen Doncaster found the last crinoline that was left; it was far too small and I had to be squeezed in by the corset. When playback was cut I continued to conduct the dances standing on a chair, in a state of total agony, with the earphones over my wig. (While shooting a dance routine the music on playback was always silenced when the scene involved dialogue.) Eventually my scene came up – I was to vamp Trevor Howard as he walked past, and all I can really remember of it was seeing the film some time later with Nigel Davenport, and his turning to me and saying, "Don't you ever do that again!" Now I am proud to have been associated at all.

The Charge of the Light Brigade was a brilliant and costly left-wing movie that didn't succeed. Since *Tom Jones*, United Artists had backed Tony both in Hollywood and in France, hoping to repeat its success. Though he was now a rich man, this pressure can't have been easy for Tony. He shrugged off the undeserved critical failure of *Charge of the Light Brigade* with his usual devil-may-care stance. *Then* it was a blow. Now the film has magnificently stood the test of time, and with its strong anti-Establishment views it has become a film that speaks clearly for the Angry Brigade of the 1950s and '60s.

Tony returned to Fielding in 1976 for his film *Joseph Andrews*. He decided that we should do our preparation work at his beautiful place in the south of France. I'd been there before, and knew what to expect. There was the usual array of incredible house guests: Nureyev, Jeremy Fry, John and Penny Mortimer, the Duke and Duchess of Suffolk, Griselda Grimond, and many other friends of both sexes. These included an Italian who dressed up in drag and sang Tosca's "Vissi d'Arte" to us all after dinner. As always, his beloved children – Natasha and Joely – were there too. Tony was a wonderful father. I don't remember working much while I was there; but he was the most generous and solicitous host. At times too solicitous.

Over dinner in a restaurant with John and Penny Mortimer, Tony said: "I think we should leave Fiz with Helen tonight, don't you, John?" John laughed. Helen was a journalist for the *Sunday Times* – later to become the fifth Mrs John Osborne.

"Why, where's Helen?" I asked somewhat fearfully.

"She's at a very nice pick-up bar in St Tropez. You know – big sailors, lorry drivers – that sort of thing. I think you'd enjoy it."

"No, I wouldn't," I said.

Tony turned plaintively to John. "I think you should try to persuade her, John–it would do her good."

John Mortimer was there to work on his life of Shakespeare with the director Peter Wood. Tony, who chose his friends with care, took agin Peter. "I think he's a dreadful man, Fiz. You know – a *bon viveur*. He uses his knowledge of wine and house decoration to be superior. There's no point to knowledge if you don't share it. I can't think why John likes him so much – it's very disappointing." One thing that was always true about Tony is that whatever he had – and he had plenty – he shared. It's a wonderful impulse, and rare.

The locations Tony chose for *Joseph Andrews*, in Bath and Gloucestershire, were ravishing. My job was to create an eighteenth-century May Day festival. I think Tony really thought this would be the other *Tom Jones* they had all waited for, but the touch had gone. I remember sitting silently at rushes with the crew roaring with laughter at a scene where Timothy West was caught shitting in a farm-yard. It wasn't funny – it was heavy-handed.

But film isn't like the theatre. You can't discuss it and go back and do it again. At his best Tony's touch was light and mercurial, and his choice of subject ambitious and exciting. Looking back, I can't help wondering whether this new heavy-handedness didn't betray a sense of desperation.

Joseph Andrews failed. Shortly afterwards Tony left for America. His hatred of England knew no bounds.

In the early '80s I went to LA to discuss with Michael Cimino the work I was to do on his film *Heaven's Gate*. Stanley drove me to the airport. "Now cut all this diffidence," he said. "The Americans don't understand it, and they don't like it." Stanley always made me laugh. And as I went through the departure gates he waved to me and said, "Remember – you have to tap dance in America!"

I was flown out first class, had a stretch-limo to meet me, and was put up at the Beverley Wiltshire Hotel. This was Hollywood! It was very exciting. I liked Michael: I had met him through Stanley, who had composed and arranged the music for Cimino's *The Deer Hunter*. Stanley's "Cavatina" – often called "The *Deer Hunter* Theme" – had become very well known. My first discussion with Michael was at his home in the Hollywood Hills. We sat in an enormous room with plush sofas in every corner. I took copious notes of what he needed for the English shoot.

Afterwards he asked me if I'd like a glass of champagne. "I'd love one," I said. And I followed him into the kitchen. He opened the door of his enormous fridge, and there was the half-bottle of champagne, and a sandwich on a plate, with a bite taken out of it. Nothing else – I've never forgotten it! It rather endeared him to me. I had no idea then that the cost of *Heaven's Gate* was to shake the whole of Hollywood and practically break United Artists.

Tony asked me to dinner while I was there. It was, as always, simple and perfect. He tried to persuade me to move to LA. "It wouldn't matter where you lived – you'd need a car, and you might have to wait a year before getting work. But it would come, and then you'd be properly paid for the first time in your life."

Wait a year for work? How would I live? No, not for me. I lack the gambling spirit – and indeed the guts – of a Tony Richardson.

Tony told me that he loved the freedom of America and the lack of class snobbery. His house was warm and unostentatious, and there were lots of guests. He still had his estate in Provence and his flat in Paris; and he told me that the only time he felt nervous was when he was flying over England – the plane might have to land. I didn't know whether to believe him or not.

In 1991 I was working at Stratford-on-Avon on Stephen Pimlott's production of *Julius Caesar*. One day in the canteen I was told I was wanted on the telephone. I recognized the caller's voice at once. "Tony, where are you?" He told me he was staying at the Athenaeum Hotel on Piccadilly and would like to see me about his forthcoming production of *The Cherry Orchard* with Vanessa. We arranged to meet at the weekend at his hotel. In the meantime I was told that he was not at all well. I was glad to have been warned, because when I arrived the designer was putting up the model of the set on the dressing-table while Tony lay in his bed.

"I want you to think up something really good for Vanessa – not just the usual family romp, but something for her to shine in."

After the designer had gone we gossiped a bit, and he made me promise to fix up my contract with the producer Robert Fox immediately. He was due to fly back to New York the next day, and had a family party that night. Going down in the lift he leaned heavily on me, and it was quite difficult to get him across the foyer where Griselda Grimond was waiting to drive him.

Not long afterwards Nic phoned me from LA to say that Tony was in hospital, seriously ill with AIDS. I asked Nic to send some flowers from me – if possible some cherry blossom.

"Mum, I don't think there's time for any of that." He was right. It was on the news the next day that Tony had died, surrounded by his daughters Natasha, Joely and Katherine, and the two women he loved, Vanessa Redgrave and Griselda Grimond. Tony was a very special man: a Socialist to the end, and from a time when theatre writers and directors used their political leanings to add a force and dimension to their creativity.

16

NO FUN WITHOUT RISK:
WILLIE DONALDSON

Accustomed to working for well-known producers, powerful and dedicated men of the theatre, I found Willie Donaldson was, to say the least, different. In a letter published in *Private Eye* he wrote: "... You did point out that I am middle-aged, balding, dishonest and unsuccessful, but you failed to mention that I masturbate, suffer from haemorrhoids, take drugs, can't satisfy my wife or anyone else and am afflicted by anxiety attacks which make my head twitch to the right at crucial moments."

Between 1961 and '71, I directed four shows for William Donaldson: *Beyond the Fringe,* starring Dudley Moore and others, *The Three Musketeers,* starring the Alberts and their children, *Nights at the Comedy,* starring Dan Farson's pub entertainers, and *Council of Love*, starring God, Mary, Jesus and Warren Mitchell as the Devil. It wasn't all easy working for Willie Donaldson but I can't say I was aware of any of the aforementioned afflictions. He was dubbed a "voyeur" – *that* I knew. His present to us after the first night of *Beyond the Fringe* was to take us to a bedroom above a hat shop in Bond Street where the milliner replaced her looking-glass with a screen, and showed us blue movies. It was an original present, but disappointingly we found it rather sick-making. I remember Peter Cook saying, "If I see that close-up once more I shall throw up on this bed."

Willie was upper class, boyishly charming, and very well educated in a non-pushy way. He was always formally dressed, usually in a pale gray suit and tie and long, dark overcoat. Behind all that, he was a man of tremendous insight who unforgivably saw the funny side of almost everything: particularly in the absurdity of pomposity. I say 'almost,' because Willie did have a short circuit. An upright and established man could put the fear of God into him. Someone like Donald Albery, say, could reduce Willie to a stuttering schoolboy. Michael Winner, on the other hand, with his Rolls Royce and fat cigars, Willie found humorous. He knew where he was and it put him at ease.

William Donaldson became an author, and a very successful one. His exposés include *Both the Ladies and the Gentlemen*, and most famously his *Henry Root Letters*. Many other novels followed, as well as a column in the *Independent*. There was a poet in Willie.

As a theatrical producer he was daring in the choice of what he put on, and always supportive and involved. One might not get paid, and never much in any case, but he was so genuinely admiring of endeavour that it almost didn't matter.

Once, after a difficult lunch with his accountant, who had apparently droned on about the problem with this country – the English don't want to work – Willie said to me, "I kept thinking about you and the Alberts slogging your guts out at the Arts. The man is a fool."

He loved the Alberts; their ingenuous anarchy delighted him. He'd put on their *British Rubbish,* and employed me to direct their *Three Musketeers* at the Arts theatre. He'd phone every night after rehearsal: "Eleanor" (Fiz would be far too familiar); "how did you get on today?" Should I ask him to a run-through, he was always there – sitting in the shadows at the back of the stalls in his long, dark overcoat, quite unperturbed by the chaos that surrounds first runs. (With the Alberts, every run.) At the end of it he'd give an intelligent and sensitive appraisal that was always encouraging. He seemed almost embarrassed to intrude.

This may not sound a great deal, but it was. An ability to be both objective and artistically involved is very unusual in a producer.

But then, of course, he wasn't a producer. His business affairs were always in a state of mayhem. And look around for him when there was trouble, and you'd be lucky to catch the exit doors still swinging from the speed of his bolting. Not infrequently he locked himself in the lavatory until either the problem was solved or the `nasty fellow' had gone away.

Avoiding a problem was Willie's only means of solving things; it didn't always work. On *Nights at the Comedy*, in which there were to be various places for audience participation – a beer-drinking competition, for example, and a talent spot, etc., the design, of necessity, included a set of stairs from the stage to the auditorium so that the audience could get up and down. Willie had failed to notify the theatre manager that a couple of rows of stalls would have to be removed for the purpose; and two days before we opened, the stairs were taken out. The show went on, but it was never what it was intended to be: a pub in a West End theatre where the audience mixed with the Music Hall acts. These included the unknown Jimmy Tarbuck, the veteran Jimmy James, Mrs Shufflewick, a Persian Princess from Ealing dancing with an enormous cobra which had a nasty habit of peeing on the stage, and the wonderful Ida Barr singing "Oh You Beautiful Doll." Dan Farson worked tirelessly bringing in his pub entertainers. He and I had scoured the working men's clubs all over the country looking for acts which we intended to change every week. We were very brave – one always was with Willie. He liked audacity and admired it as though there was something pure about it, or purifying.

It may have been his production of *Council of Love*, which I directed with Jack Gold in 1970, that saw Willie out of the theatre. It very nearly saw me into prison.

The play was written by Oscar Panizza at the turn of the century. Recently it had been successfully revived in

Paris, where Willie saw it and bought the rights. He got John Bird to do a translation, which Jack Gold found more serious than the French version. There were two scenes in Heaven with God, Mary, Jesus and the Devil, which Jack Gold was to direct, and two at the Borgia's Vatican for me with a cast of twenty-seven: popes, wrestlers, dancers, etc. These orgy scenes were to be erotic and provide the argument of the play: i.e., whether God or the Devil takes responsibility for social and/or moral evils. In other words, I was lumbered.

"Willie, you'll have to help me," I said, aware that he knew about orgies. "I mean, what happens?"

"I'm fastidious about beginning mine in a very formal way," Willie said. "Evening dress, butlers, white table-cloths...." Willie laughed and turned a little pink.

"Yes. Then what?"

"Then the door bell might ring. There'll be something strange about this late arrival; perhaps a woman in a decolletée dress with a chipmunk on her shoulder."

"A chipmunk?"

"I have a great respect for those dashing little creatures; they rush about biting people in inappropriate places." Willie laughed again, too embarrassed to go on. "Good Heavens, Eleanor – you've got it made. You're starting at the Vatican!"

It wasn't much help, but it was something. Adding to my difficulties was the fact that we had omitted to have an Equity representative at the dancers' auditions, which meant that none of them could remove a stitch of their 1490 clothing. With such a large cast we assumed we'd be going to a large theatre, but half way through rehearsal we were informed by the four producers (Willie had added a few friends: Donald Langdon, Anthony Perry and a Frenchman called Jean Leyris) that we would be going to the Criterion – a tiny stage that involved a lot of re-designing and re-thinking. Jack Gold, used to the camera, finished his rehearsals in a few days; he thought he'd be able to edit later. Meanwhile I battled on in search of erotica. Only the end worked: a dancer standing on the Pope's throne with a wrestler clutching her knees and the last Bishop turning round to watch as she starts to unbutton her bodice.

The critic B. A. Young wrote that the show made *Oh Calcutta* seem sophisticated. Anyway, he doubted its power to affect a British audience: "To care about an assault on the Church, you must first care about the church. Panizza went to prison for blasphemy when the play was first produced. How many people have been sent to prison for blasphemy in Great Britain?" He spoke too soon.

Some time into the run, after I had put in two nude dancers (as Willie and his friends felt the audience were going away disappointed), the phone rang at home. It was the *Sunday Express*.

"Nigel, it's for you," I called out. I was living with Nigel Davenport.

"No," he returned. "It's for you."

"Miss Fazan?"

"Yes."

"May we have your comments on being served a petition for blasphemy?"

"I'm sorry – I don't know what you're talking about."

"You don't know?"

"Know what?"

"Lady Birdwood has brought out a private petition against you and Jack Gold for blasphemy."

Blasphemy is a criminal charge. I phoned John Mortimer immediately.

Willie and his four friends were nowhere to be found. Every day I expected Willie to phone: "Eleanor, what's that dear old baggage Lady Birdwood been up to today?" He never did.

To cut a long story short, we were tried at Bow Street Magistrates' Court. John was brilliant. He arrived late, his wig a little squiffy, his gown flowing and an entourage in pursuit. I was so relieved to see him. He had previously warned me that when he'd been asked if his client (me) was the Eleanor Fazan who had co-directed *Council of Love* at the Criterion, he had replied, "We admit nothing." This apparently meant that someone would be brought in to point me out. I wondered who the dirty turn-coat might be. It was the stage-manager, who despite his short sight and shaking hand managed to do the deed. His presence gave the clever John someone to question.

"You are the stage-manager of *Council of Love*, are you not?"

"Oh yes."

"Then you will know, will you not, that on the date Lady Birdwood attended this show, Miss Fazan was away in Nottingham, working on a production at the Nottingham Playhouse."

"Oh yes."

Pandemonium broke out. Surely I couldn't be held responsible for what was going on on stage if I was miles away. Such was their ignorance of the theatre!

The case was dismissed with costs.

Neither John Mortimer, nor my solicitor Michael Oliver, charged me a penny. I owe them a great debt. Had the case gone on to the criminal court, I could have been in for thousands and would undoubtedly have chosen prison. Michael Oliver told me that Lady Birdwood's counsel thought I should get off as I had sat up as straight as a die throughout the proceedings. (I was petrified.)

Fifteen years later a dancer bought me a paperback book. It was called *Great Disasters of the Stage*, and it was written by William Donaldson.

"You're in it," he said. Under a chapter called "God's Mysterious Ways," I read:

When Oscar Panizza's irreligious satire, Council d'Amour, *was presented at the tiny Criterion Theatre in 1970 the producers had got their arithmetic wrong. The cast— God, fairies, randy cardinals, wrestlers, nudes, popes, Christ, tumblers, girls nobbing from nowhere to bite one another in the box — was so extensive that the play would have lost £4000 a week playing to capacity. The larger the audience, paradoxically, the more quickly the producers would have gone bankrupt. God intervened on their behalf. The Dowager Lady Birdwood — enthusiastically seconded by Lord Ampthill, heir to the grocery millions — brought a private prosecution under the 1376 Blasphemy Act, by which, if found guilty, the play's blameless choreographer, the great and wonderful Eleanor Fazan, would have been burnt at the stake as a witch. John Mortimer appeared, as so often, for the accused, the action failed humiliatingly and old Lady Birdwood was rebuked by the magistrate (George Robey's grandson, as it happened) for wasting the court's time. Meanwhile, the play, which was clearly in contempt of court, had been withdrawn, allowing the producers to escape with their fancy women to Morocco, where they opened a pub selling Watney's Red Barrel.*

17

ECCENTRIC VIRTUE:
BARRY HUMPHRIES

Australians seem to me to have one thing in common: they collect things. Books, paintings, people, names, recipes, machines – everything, really; yet this is a side of their nature they prefer not to recognise. Bruce Beresford, the Australian film director, told me that the comedian Barry Humphries had telephoned him from Australia to ask him to clear up his London flat. "There was junk all over the place," Bruce said. "Jewelry under the bed, videos in the bath – paintings and records just lying around. How could anyone treat their possessions in such a way?"

I had first met Barry Humphries when he was playing Mr Sowerberry the undertaker in Lionel Bart's *Oliver!* It was a small part and Barry was rather too much all over the place to make much impression, but the job probably suited him. It would have given him the time to mix around, go to exhibitions, do his weekly cartoon of Barry MacKenzie for *Private Eye*, and plan his one-man show for Australia.

Barry was a tall, lanky figure with a lean aesthetic face and long, straight hair before it was fashionable. He was usually dressed in white. Whether it was tee shirt and shorts, or well-cut tropical suit, it would be white. Whenever I bumped into him, I was always terribly aware of his extreme intelligence, all-piercing eyes, and eccentricity. Eccentric, not dotty or anti-conformist, and disarmingly so. Rather as Dryden explained when he wrote: "A character of eccentric virtue is the more exact image of human life because it is not wholly exempt from its frailties." Barry certainly was not exempt from frailties, and he went on to build a brilliant career satirising the frailties of others.

In 1969 Barry was again in London, and he asked me if I would direct his one-man show for the Fortune Theatre. As it happened we shared the same agent. It was quite crafty of him to push me for the job because a director was hardly necessary. The show had already been a big success in Australia with only a stage manager in charge. But I knew how to get a show on in London; and more importantly, when to leave well alone. Being there had its uses too, not least because Barry was drinking; the falling-in-the-ditch kind of drinking.

The show, called *Just a Show*, consisted of a series of one-man character sketches, each one brilliantly observed.

There was Rex Lear, a philistine, *nouveau-riche* father at his daughter's wedding, drunk on champagne and throwing up in the flower arrangements; Martin Agrippa, a bearded underground movie director; Neil Singleton, a pseudo-intellectual giving a party in his Tai Wan-decorated flat; Sandy Stone, the boring, self-pitying patient in a wheelchair; Nipper Dixon, the beach boy chundering (Australian for throwing up) on his prawns and Fosters lager; and lastly, Mrs Edna Everage on her first disapproving visit to London, throwing gladioli into the audience to bring a little life to the half-dead pommies.

As it was necessary to have something happen during Barry's changes, we advertised in *The Stage* for an organist. Josie Bradley replied, and Barry and I went together to North Finchley to hear her play on the organ in her dining room. She was perfect. Dressed to the nines in a pink spot with a huge glass of brandy to hand, Josie entertained the audience between sketches by thumping out old 'forties tunes. The show was wonderfully tacky.

Virtually unknown to the British public, Barry was interviewed on TV during our final technical rehearsal. When I got home around midnight, there he was, still in full costume from the TV show, with his girlfriend Ros, knocking back the booze with Nigel. None of them had met before, but Barry had called round to hear how things had gone for me. Nigel told me later that he had laughed so much watching Barry give Joan Bakewell the giggles on TV, that he'd fallen asleep in front of the box. He was woken by the doorbell. "There in the doorway stood this man in a pink frock and high heels requesting a Fernet

Branca. It's not all easy living with you, Fazan," Nigel said. He drove them back eventually to their Bayswater Hotel, none too sober himself. Apparently Barry had jumped out of the car full of beans, waved "So long, Nigel" at the window, and still in his pink frock, straw hat and high heels, keeled over in one straight piece into the gutter.

Advertisement for Barry Humphries' "Just a Show" (Before Edna had become a Dame)

Just a Show was superb in its way, and some people came back several times–but not the critics. One wrote: "Mr Humphries embraces the lowest common denominator much in the Blackpool Summer Show way – picking on late comers, doling out gladioli for everyone to make lewd gestures with, leading a jolly song or two. If it's satirical as the camp transformation into Edna Everage might lead you to suspect, then it's so heavy handed and overblown that it's really way out." He felt that *Just a Show* was as it claimed, just that, "with nothing particular to recommend it."

Today – though I regret that most of Barry's inspired characters have long since gone – his waspish Edna Everage, now the viperish Dame Edna – soon to become Saint Edna – fills every house alone and the rich and famous flock to be 'picked on' as they lewdly wave their gladioli in hope of Barry's (or Dame Edna's) attention. "Sad little people," Dame Edna calls them.

To go from Edna Everage in 1969 to the celebration of Dame Edna today cannot have been easy. Journalists wonder if Barry and Edna have become one and the same person – the ventriloquist's dummy having taken over the ventriloquist. This sounds far-fetched to me because having worked with Barry, it is the man of eccentric virtue that I most remember: in particular his pronounced personal loathing of anyone who grew fat off others. That a producer should get rich off *his* creativity (or anyone else's, for that matter) rankled deeply, and he was determined to be able to do without them. Indeed he was at pains to recognise and protect himself from what he called the "con-men."

Driving through St John's Wood in the mid-'70's, he said: "I always wish I had a gun with me when I'm driving through this neck of the woods. I'd like to shoot at all those psychiatrists who took thousands of pounds off me while I was drinking. There's one," he said, pointing at a window, "and there's another. The only way to stop drinking is to stop drinking." He had, and was now working tirelessly for those who hadn't. I asked him if he would see a friend of mine, and he suggested we go straight away. I explained she might not be in, as I knew she was seeing her analyst that day. "Then she'll be really smashed," Barry said. When we got there, she was lying in front of the gas fire in her bikini. Barry found this perfectly understandable and chatted to her with great dignity and care.

Once, when I was driving my son back to Oxford where he was taking his A levels, Barry came with us to keep me company on the way back. Watching Nic wave us goodbye from his rather dismal digs was too much for Barry. Unbeknownst to me, while I was away touring with the Prospect Company, Barry got Nic up to London and gave him an enormous blow-out lunch at Simpsons.

There was an old ex-dancer whom Barry had met in Australia – a friendly but terrible winger who lived miles away in Barnet and moaned about lack of work. Quite often we met there for supper. On the last visit, Barry said on the way back, "What is it about me that makes me collect these hopeless people?" He made me laugh, but I knew he was bothered by it and had the strong feeling all this would change. He was too ambitious. Not for himself, but rather to beat the monsters at their own game.

It was the films that he made with Bruce Beresford, based on his cartoons of Barry MacKenzie with himself as MacKenzie's Aunt Edna, that eventually brought him the public acclaim that he needed and he hasn't looked back.

Now Barry can do as he pleases. He is married for the third or fourth time and frequently appears on TV. He collects works of art – something he always had an eye for, and a brilliant eye. I've noticed that eye is also searing when collecting money for the handicapped.

Barry Humphries is my idea of the Renaissance Man – someone whose nature drives him to experience at first hand, to gain understanding from that experience. At one time it nearly did him in. Luckily though, he was saved by his extraordinary intelligence which willed him to use his anger creatively. The venomous Dame Edna deserves to become a saint.

18

STAR TURN:
ALEC GUINNESS

In 1973 the producer Michael Codron asked me to choreograph various numbers for Alan Bennett's play *Habeas
Corpus*. During rehearsals Alec Guinness, who was playing
the lead, took me aside one day, and asked if he could have
a private word with me. As I followed him down the corridor I wondered what this might mean.

Turning to me, Sir Alec looked deadly serious and
spoke in his low, quiet voice. He told me that he was not
happy with the end of the play as written.

"I've done endless death scenes, and I'm sick of them.
I should like to end the play with a Dance of Death. Are
you up for it?"

I gulped. You can't play around with a star of his calibre. I would have to come up with an idea that was not only right for the play but suitable for him; one that made him look good as a dancer. A tall order. I'd already noticed he was a bit doddery when he hopped.

Sir Alec continued, "We'll have to rehearse after hours and in secret. That way if the dance doesn't work no one need know anything about it. If it does – then leave it to me."

What he didn't tell me was that he had already discussed the idea of a dance with Michael, Alan and the director Ronald Eyre, and it had gone down like a lead balloon. Vetoed, in fact!

I went ahead and hired a rehearsal room, and asked Brian Stamborough, a brilliant pianist for the Royal Opera House, to play for us; the business of getting the music onto tape could come later, once it was fixed.

People seem to think that choreographers simply get to rehearsal and unpack the choreography. Not so. We think, think, think; worry, worry, worry; visualize in our heads; until something starts to take shape in our mind's eye. And even then we must be ready to change and alter at rehearsal according to the people, or person, we are working with.

In this instance, and because he had to perform to taped music, I dreamed up the idea of having the tape stop at a certain moment in the dance and wind back – Sir Alec winding back with it. Each time the dance re-started the tape would stop a little earlier before winding back, until in the end he was stuck in a groove endlessley repeating the same lift of a leg as the lights faded.

Sir Alec seemed to like this idea, and so we started work. He was meticulous in getting every step just right, including all the reversed steps on the wind-backs, and was indeed a pleasure to work with. Quite often he'd go to Brian's house after work to put in some extra rehearsals. Only when he was entirely confident of his performance did he take over.

The next thing I knew we were rehearsing on stage. The "Dance of Death" was to end the play. Sir Alec had got his way!

Well, Alec Guinness was a Star. And like every Star I have ever met, male or female, he was strategic.

We opened out of town, and the dance was a hit. As the curtain came down I saw Michael Codron run past me in the stalls to congratulate the author and director for ending the play so successfully. No one said anything to me. At the warm-up for the West End opening Ron Eyre told the assembled company that I had taken the idea for Alec's dance from Laurel and Hardy. News to me! Just why he should say such a thing is a mystery. The stage-manager thought Ron Eyre had wanted to try to belittle the dance because he was angry with Alec Guinness for pulling off an idea he had vetoed.

It doesn't matter. As a choreographer you have to find the ironic shrug. You know that even those in our profession have no idea what it takes to choreograph.

(printed by permission of Penguin Books)

Alec Guinness performing "The Dance of Death".

I did not go to the opening night. I did what I always do when I need to pick myself up and dust myself down: I went home. My trick for survival.

I'm happiest working with dancers. On a TV production of *Scarlet and Black* I was asked to arrange a quadrille for the ballroom scene. This dance, for some twenty-four dancers, was to be reflected in a mirror in front of which two actors were to play their scene. This scene took a great many takes, and on every single one the dancers, who stood little chance of being seen at all, gave their all, as dancers always do. In the break I told them all how fantastic I thought they were.

"Oh good," said one. "Shall we go on tour?" We all laughed.

It was very typical. Dancers work without fear and without reproach. For that alone, they represent all that is most noble in our profession.

19

GERMAN GENIUS: GŐTZ FRIEDRICH

I was in Floral Street outside the RSC rehearsal room when I was startled by a colleague I hadn't seen for some time.

"What are you doing standing here in the street – alone?" he asked.

"If you really want to know," I replied, "I'm trying to screw up the courage to go in to work."

He looked amazed. "That's not like you, surely?"

"Well, it is now," I said, and it was true. I was going through a bad patch both at home and at work. Not through lack of work – there was plenty – but because compared to my colleagues (who were, on the whole, all men) I had always been so poorly paid. I felt bitter and twisted. It seemed to me that I had given far more than I had ever taken; and now, quite suddenly, I was sick of it all. I wanted OUT.

It was no surprise to me when my agent gave me the push. The reason was that I didn't comply with the William Morris rule of having to make ten thousand a year – I was hard pushed to make between three and four.

However, I was surprised to find the musician Alan Price sitting on a wall outside the entrance as I slunk out. I sat on the wall beside him and told him what had just happened.

"Whew!" he whistled. "The cold, harsh winds are blowing, Fiz."

I laughed as I went home. Had he sympathised I might have burst into tears.

A few days later, on March 26 1974 – twenty-nine years to the day since I had left Africa – I received a telephone call from a man called Elijah Moshinsky on behalf of the Royal Opera House. He explained he was the assistant of Herr Professor Götz Friedrich, who, with the Music Director Colin Davis, would be producing a new Ring Cycle at Covent Garden in the autumn. Mr Moshinsky wished to interview me, not as a choreographer, but as someone who would fit in with a director's ideas and handle any movement that might be required. Delia Lyndon, a stage-manager there, had apparently suggested me. I remembered Delia as a dancer in *Jack and the Beanstalk* – a pantomime I'd done at Windsor, which hardly seemed auspicious for an assignment that sounded so grand; but thanks to her recommendation, and the fact that I'd worked with Barry Humphries (Mr Moshinsky, it transpired, was Australian) I landed my first job in Grand Opera. It was a world I knew nothing about; but something new and difficult was exactly what I needed. It couldn't have come at a better time. Who, for a start, was Herr Professor Götz Friedrich?

Opera Director, Götz Friedrich, 1980s

First and most important, Götz Friedrich was a German artist of great stature: soon to be the Intendant, or Artistic Director, of the Berlin Opera House. The son of a barrister, he was born in Naumberg in 1930. When Germany was divided at the end of the war, Friedrich found himself, perhaps fortunately, in the GDR. As a young student of theatre studies, he was taken up by the legendary Walter Felsenstein of the Komische Oper in East Berlin, with whom he remained for twenty years. "I owe almost everything to him," Friedrich said in an interview. "It was from him that I learned to analyse the dramatic structure of a work, both from its music and its text, and, where possible, to find a basic idea to express in a text."

In the same interview Friedrich went on to explain the necessary search for a "concept." He saw it as a means of making what was probably a nineteenth-century piece accessible to today's audience. David Pountey's *Carmen* is a car-park, or Jonathan Miller's *Rigoletto* among the Mafia, would be clear examples. The opera director, it would seem to me, is drawn to "Conceptual Theatre" because – apart from staging and keeping an overall eye on the *mise en scène* – he is not really needed. The composer has already dictated the emotional content of a piece in his music, and it is the conductor who is in charge of those dynamics. The singers come to rehearsal knowing their roles – probably they have played them several times before – and it is the conductor whom they look to first; it is his interpretation of the music that is going to make or break their performance. And it is the conductor who has the deciding vote on whether or not a singer is cast. But because operas have become such vast and costly undertakings, the director, providing he is a strong and autocratic operator, is assured of his position. A strong concept makes him indispensable.

"It doesn't matter what people do in my productions," Götz once told me, and I didn't understand him. But then I wasn't used to "Conceptual Theatre." In opera, a director's concept must be approved by the conductor and then fed to the designer, often two years before rehearsals begin. Rehearsals themselves are to a large extent a matter of accommodation. If the Nibelungen, as the "oppressed", are dressed as little ants, one must make sure the movement is in keeping. This doesn't make the rehearsals any easier – far from it. Inspiration comes from the orchestra-pit and the singers. Production values are there to enhance it. "Conceptual Theatre" is not an art that conceals itself. It's there for all to see; the art is in the pre-planning. All this I was to learn by degrees.

Colin Davis told me early on, "All this work we are doing won't make a blind bit of difference, you know. You'll be very disappointed. You'll look up there on the opening night and see them sitting in the Grand Tier with their medals, and do you know what they'll be saying? 'Ah, but I remember Birgit Nilsson as Brunhilde,' or 'What a pity you didn't hear Hans Hotter's Wotan.' Canary collectors – all of them. Gynecologists mostly."

I felt enormously relieved.

I had all summer to prepare myself for this epic of four operas, without the slightest idea of what would be expected of me. Götz Friedrich would not be in London until just before rehearsals began. Betty Scholar, Colin Davis's PA, fed me with as much information as was available: we were to get six Rhinemaiden doubles, forty children as Nibelungen, and twenty-eight actors. It was apparently taken for granted that the director would approve our choice. I was constantly out of my depth.

Opera people talk opera all the time, referring to "Act Three Valkure" or "the Immolation scene," as though the reference was obvious. I would rush home at night to struggle with Wagner and the tapes I'd made from records borrowed from the library. To help me, Betty arranged that I should see the English National Opera Company's *Rheingold* and *Valkure* in Birmingham: their length and boredom shook me rigid. So did the Wagnerites and their picnic baskets. I stayed up there with a relation of Stanley's, and I don't think anything has ever tasted as good as the chicken soup she had waiting for me when I got back from the theatre. The poor darling had waited up for hours.

"Don't worry, dear – I expect you'll get used to it," she said, and I laughed.

"Please God I shall live that long, Auntie Ray!"

My first introduction to Herr Professor Götz Friedrich was, of necessity, brief. Apart from a poem which began "*Ich frage die Maus, Wo ist dein Haus?*" ("I asked the mouse, where is your house?") I had no German whatsoever, and at that time Götz spoke no English. It was a few days before rehearsals began, and we were at a Sitz-Bauer, or scenery rehearsal. Götz sat at the Production desk, chain-smoking and shouting instructions in German. Sitting in the darkness of the vast Covent Garden auditorium, I watched with amazement the entire stage rise up on its central pillar, swivel a couple of times, and tilt away from the audience to reveal an underside clad entirely in mirrors. Friedrich's concept for the Ring Cycle was "To get away from the myth element and hold up a mirror to the world". Hmm, I could see what he meant: there were mirrors everywhere!

Quite suddenly I received a tap on the shoulder; would I go down to the basement stage and rehearse the children for Scene Two? Professor Friedrich wanted to test our reflections in the mirror.

If ever I have wanted to die, I did at that moment. Clearly I was supposed to know what happens, or at least to have pre-planned the whole thing.

I followed the ballet mistress, Romayne Grigorova, to where the forty children were waiting, feeling quite sick; and with nothing but "The Oppressed" in my head, I took a deep breath and began. I shoved the children through Chain Gang, Union meetings, workers being whipped, workers fainting, bludgeoned and carried out dead. I went on and on and on, until Romayne touched my arm and pointed up on stage. There, surrounded by his minions, discussing some prop, was Götz Friedrich. Clearly he hadn't been watching us.

"*Kannen wir halten jetz?*" (Can we stop now?) Romayne asked; and Götz waved a dismissive hand.

A small black boy ran over to me, panting. "Have we got the job, Miss?"

I didn't know. We didn't seem to matter much.

"You were fabulous," I said.

Rehearsals began with the Rhinemaidens. I still hadn't had any discussion with my director. He stood, a large and passionate man, score in hand, in the centre of the complicated set of steps and troughs which masked the vast stage machinery, around which the Rhinemaidens were to sing and dance gracefully while reflected by mirrors into the audience. This was some feat. Götz however was quick and decisive.

"Wellgunde, kommen Sie hier: Flossie das Geld shauen Sie. Woglinde, gehen Sie Weg. ELEENOR!"

I jumped to my feet. The shouted ELEENOR meant that a singer had gone off; I must shove on a dancer double. And I did just that, making up something on the spur of the moment. By the end of the day, Götz had blocked Scene One. I had no idea what anyone had done, and nor had any of them.

I learned in time it was best just to watch Götz, get as much down on paper as I could, and then later sort it all out and alter my own work. This seemed to suit Götz, and amazingly we got on well: partly, I think, because he didn't think much of the English, and as I was from Kenya I was somewhat absolved. He would break off while explaining something, to say, "Of course you English have no interest in History." And later, on his *Elektra* production in Vienna, when I'd sneaked out to watch the Royal wedding on TV, Götz shouted out, "Hasn't their television broken down yet? The English can never make anything work."

No one ever replied. In opera the hierarchy is maintained. The bosses get away with murder if so inclined.

Early on Elijah Moshinsky phoned to tell me that Götz had said there were too may Jews in the Opera House. I asked him to stop telling me these horrors. "I have to work with him," I said. And I meant it. I liked Götz – or I wanted to. I certainly admired him. Of course between us there was the unwritten law of the theatre that you never get too close to your colleagues.

I loved watching Götz rehearse. No one could say he was not a brilliant opera director: a workaholic with a total grasp of the whole. He worked in the true German tradition: he was an Expressionist. He explored the predicaments of symbolic types – flinging himself against a rock as Siegelinde, or, as Brunhilde, falling crushed into submission at the feet of Wotan; responding ecstatically to the music: "*Ja, ja, das ist schön!*"

When he couldn't get his way he would walk out; always smoking, and driving himself in the search for visual equivalents for passionate feelings. Usually this involved blood. This was my first experience of the German artist, and I wondered if they were all as passionate and tyrannical.

No one can live long at such high intensity. After a while it becomes monstrous. If Götz, as an Expressionist, had divorced Art from Realism, he had also divorced himself from normal human contact. Try saying, "How are you, Götz?" and you'd be ignored; work hard, and he was appreciative in his own way. To think of him as lonely was mere sentimentality, but I did.

Although Colin Davis had had such high hopes of this collaboration with Friedrich, he was the first to balk. On *Der Freischutz* three years later, in 1977, he came up to me and said, "Has Götz shouted at you today?"

"Not yet," I replied. "But any moment now, I suspect." We were all pretty used to it.

"Well, let me know if he does. I've had enough of all this shouting. I can't stand it any more."

Although he was not to leave the Opera House until 1986, Sir Colin Davis did not work with Friedrich again.

With Colin's departure the last vestiges of the Opera House as a democratic workplace went too. No more sitting on the floor in his office sorting out the rehearsal schedule with him. No more auditioning with the ballet-master Leslie Edwards and Romayne Grigorova and having our choice automatically accepted. Now it was rows of offices, admin, and departments: far less personal and not necessarily more efficient.

Nothing, though, could have prepared me for Vienna. Götz had asked me to work there on his film of *Elektra*. In July 1981 he was happily married to the soprano Karen Armstrong, and their new son delighted him. But his newfound happiness didn't seem to have changed the way he worked.

I was asked to find out how many of the women extras would agree to appear in the nude during my rehearsals for Clytemnestra's orgy. As extra money was involved, they all agreed. This meant they must be lined up, stripped to the waist, so that Götz and his designer might choose the best endowed.

They stopped in front of each girl in turn. "*Nicht!*" The girl's face fell.

"*Nicht! ... Ja ... ja ... Nicht!*"

And so on, down the line.

It was a humiliating sight. But then their treatment was humiliating altogether. No one cared about the hours they were kept, how frozen they became being hosed down in simulated rain, take after take. Tea breaks, or breaks of any sort, Götz had always called "English bourgeois shit," and it seemed there was nothing to protect them in Vienna.

Those that received the "*Ja*" vote were herded into a blood bath and stripped off. Buckets of red gunge were flung over them as they dutifully squirmed and squealed for the cameras. "*Mehr Blut, mehr Blut!*" (More blood!) Götz was still shouting as I left for my hotel.

Götz staged this *Elektra* for the opera House in 1990. At the first gathering Götz said, "Look at Eleenor – she doesn't know whether she is doing Eletra's dance or not."

I smiled at him. I no longer jumped.

In the event, Elektra's dance was scrapped in favour of smearing the stage with blood. I had to choreograph a sacrificial tribal dance on a high rostrum behind closed shutters. Götz had insisted that I put three nudes among the twenty-four dancers. This offended Sir Georg Solti – hence the shutters. At least so I was told; it was not discussed with me.

At my last rehearsal the stage director, Stella Chitty, caught me before I went in.

"Oh, Eleanor, you might like to know Götz was terribly sweet last night at the lighting rehearsal. He kept thumping his desk and shouting "I WANT ELEENOR UP THERE – NUDE!"

"Oh my God, Stella – that doesn't bode too well!" I said; and she looked rather crushed.

It was too late for me to explain... As I ran in Gotz called me over to sit beside him, while he made some changes. I loved to watch him work. Brilliant – *ja*; talented – *ja, ja*, sexual, hard-working passionate, tyrannical, unstinting of himself – *ja, ja, ja*. But "sweet"? GŐTZ? Never. Not his style.

20

THE GRIZZLY BEAR: YURI LYUBIMOV

In 1986, when Zurich Opera House rang to say that Yuri Lyubimov had asked them to engage me as choreographer on his forthcoming production of *Jenufa*, I had to ask around, "Who is he... ?" Somehow I had not been aware of his production of *Crime and Punishment* at the Lyric Hammersmith, for which this defecting director of the Tanganka Theatre in Moscow had won high praise from the London critics the year before. My friends too were vague, but of one thing they seemed certain: Lyubimov was a genius; so I set off to Frankfurt where he was working, ready for our first meeting, full of enthusiasm and anticipation.

My flight was delayed and I arrived at the block of flats where we were to meet two hours late. However, Mr Lyubimov, looking like a large, crumpled Russian bear, arrived four hours late; he had been held up at rehearsal by conflict with the choreographer. My heart sank as we followed Tatiana, his interpreter, up the concrete stairs to her one-room apartment.

Tatiana sat on the bed looking rather like Giselle's mother, Lyubimov on the one chair, and I on the bathroom stool. He spoke only Russian, so we communicated through Tatiana. I noticed he fingered the score nervously. He surprised me by launching into an outline of the story. Any questions, I was told, would all be answered by a Paul Hernan in London, who as it turned out lived quite close to me. As he was leaving Lyubimov turned at the door and asked me to be very exigent about selecting the movement group. What movement group? Where? How many? About twelve to twenty. Paul Hernan would fill me in.

I stayed on to try to glean a little more from Tatiana. Apparently Stefan Lazaridis had originally designed the production, and it was he that had recommended me; but there had been some tremendous row. Stefan had walked out and his assistant had taken over. Tatiana was concerned only for Lyubimov: "Poor Yuri, how could he cope with the sophistication of Lazaridis – it's just not possible."

I returned to London and phoned Zurich. They were horrified by the thought of twelve extra people, and they asked me if I would take on the responsibility of choosing them. It took three trips to Zurich to get what I hoped was right; and in the meantime I went to see Paul Hernan.

Paul had the model of the set in his house, and a strong grasp of the way the production would take shape. He had directed Opera himself in Ireland. He marked my score exactly where the movement group would move the scenery, told me they'd be used at the start of each act, and as a shadow group with "moral undertones" in various other places. I must have turned green, for he said: "You mean he didn't tell you?"

"No. It doesn't matter. Do you know how or where?"

"Not really. But don't worry. Yuri really prefers to do these things himself."

I was relieved to hear this, but wary. I'd been caught that way before. In my job it's essential to understand the vision of the director in order to prepare oneself. It's a process. So often you are expected to do instant choreography; and unless you have prepared yourself correctly it seldom works well.

I arrived in Zurich in some trepidation, the day before rehearsal. I was given the keys to my apartment, which I was told was *gemütlich*, as it had an open fire. It was in a block in the drug district and had lots of burnt-down candles, a guitar on the wall and a pile of plastic children's toys in the corner. Not cheap, either.

The next day we all met in the chorus rehearsal room. Paul Hernan explained the model of the set. Lyubimov, spruce now in a white polo-necked jersey and dark Italian glasses, once more gave an outline of the story of *Jenufa*. Bemused rather than insulted, the cast waited patiently. He told us that tragedy perpetuates itself; one drunk or suicide, for example, in a small village can cause a devastation that will be felt for generations. Everyone was then dismissed except myself and the movement group. At last, I hoped, it would become clear what the director expected; but his instructions were simply to "move around." They all looked at me in terror.

This kind of generalised direction is always unnerving. I guessed that Lyubimov needed to see what the group could do, so I suggested we take up the theme of his talk: a small community going happily about their tasks, some preparing a bride for her wedding; when the bridegroom enters, he's drunk; and as he moves amongst them, they either join him, or their mood changes to despair. They managed extremely well. Lyubimov jumped to his feet, offered profuse congratulations and told them he would be relying heavily on them during the production. They were charmed. He then showed them how each act would begin: Act One, chucking seeds for Spring; Act Two, chucking leaves for Autumn; and Act Three, chucking snow for Winter. He encouraged them with one repeated instruction: "*Plastisish, plastisish.*"

Mr Lyubimov is a wonderful performer and a marvellous mime; this is the secret of his success. Unfortunately he is performing all the time and you can never find a centre with which to communicate. Also his performance as director (the shouting/screaming sort) makes any communication well nigh impossible. Before he left, I asked if that chucking step was all he wanted, or whether I could develop it with some variation. He shouted at me in Russian which I took to mean, "Are you some kind of idiot?" and started the tape recorder. He repeated the chucking seeds step for Spring and I whispered to Tatiana, "But this is the music for Act Three." She nodded and smiled affectionately. "You know these geniuses," she said without a trace of irony. I nodded and smiled back.

By the time the first chorus session came, we were used to the singers going through their parts and improvising their moves while Tatiana whispered in Lyubimov's ear what was supposed to be going on. Once he'd got the hang of it, he'd get up and act out each part extremely well to the great joy of some, though less for others. This technique does not work with a large chorus, and when their music cue came, nothing happened. They waited for instruction.

Apart from their dance, I had not been asked to work with the chorus; but like an idiot, I leapt up to help. I placed the villagers, brought on the recruits and got Jenufa to look among them for Steva. Tatiana went on whispering. Suddenly Lyubimov slammed his hand on his desk and roared with laughter. Only an English 'Imperialist,' he said (meaning me), would grab someone by the hand. My ploy to save the day for Lyubimov was a failure. After his outburst against me, he sat back and continued to say nothing. Before the session ended, and quite suddenly, a brave and very frustrated member of the chorus stepped forward, and alone, in the middle of the floor, he told Lyubimov he should go up to the Swiss mountains for at least five months and study the score of *Jenufa*. The whole company was stunned by his courage; the outburst cost him his job.

It was Paul Herman who really got the show up and running. He was grateful for the huge responsibility he had been given, and worked like a slave. Especially at night, when Lyubimov would take Tatiana back to their hotel to work on his immigration papers. He planned to become a Zurich citizen, for tax purposes. Their absence gave Paul the chance to light the production in peace and quiet.

I never cease to be amazed at the way the wheels of opera turn. It can encompass almost anything, and the Operhaus Zurich is a long-established house.

For me it was a personal hell, and to this day I'm not sure how I stuck it out. After each orchestral rehearsal I'd screw up the courage to ask Lyubimov if he had any instructions or alterations for me. He would either wave his hand as though brushing off a flea, or shout at me in Russian with such vituperation that the interpreters would hang their heads, no doubt hoping I wouldn't ask them to interpret! I was lucky to have a lot of rehearsals to myself, but even then more than once I looked round to see Lyubimov mimicking my every move. Probably very well too.

I watched the final dress rehearsal with interest. The chorus was simple and excellent, and the movement group, confident now from our long rehearsals together, were exemplary. They showed the influence of the director, as did the principals, who performed not as people caught in a personal tragedy, but as puppets in the hands of Fate. This was Lyubimov's contribution; a concept he would endeavour to impose on anything.

I was sitting one day in the canteen, wishing I was rich enough to walk out, when Tatiana came to join me. Her eyes were filled with tears. *Jenufa* had been delayed a week and now she had to leave for her next job at NATO. Lyubimov had yelled at her. "He told me: 'The only thing you people in the West think about is MONEY!'... and I've worked so hard for him."

I said, "All that work you do for him at night on his tax papers – does he ever pay you?"

She shook her head.

"A bunch of flowers?" She started to cry.

"Well, I wouldn't worry about it, Tatiana. Just be glad you have another job, and let's hope at NATO there isn't a single genius in sight!" It didn't help. Poor Tatiana wanted to believe what she wanted to believe. She's not alone.

When I returned to London after several weeks in Amsterdam on Wagner's *Maestersingers*, I discovered that Covent Garden had bought our Zurich production of *Jenufa*. They had been a little surprised by the fact that Lyubimov had stated he did not want me to be involved, and Richard Gregson from the production office was detailed to take me to lunch and question me on how it had been in Zurich. I told him that Paul Hernan had got the show on the road and that, apart from being a highly gifted actor and mime, Lyubimov as a director seemed to me to be what we call "out of it."

No one took any notice of what I said, for the next thing I heard was that the Opera House had taken the extraordinary step of booking Lyubimov to direct their forthcoming Ring Cycle. Well... within three weeks from the start of rehearsals the Opera House knew the *Ring* was never going to work with Yuri Lubimov. After *Rheingold* they gave him the push, *and* at vast expense to themselves.

Moral: Always listen to the choreographer! We have so little to lose!

21

THE MENSCH AND THE MAESTRO:
JOHN SCHLESINGER and
HERBERT VON KARAJAN

Whenever I see a Father Christmas I think of John Schlesinger, for that is how he looked when I first met him in 1977. He was somewhat chubby, with a neat white beard, a cherubic smile, and sparkling blue eyes. Also he loved to laugh a lot – not so much "Ho, ho, ho!" but at camp jokes – high camp jokes – which could make his whole body shake with mirth. John was a happy homosexual. He was also "a gent."

I had known of him, of course. Often on a Sunday night Stanley and I would watch *Monitor*, a BBC TV show for which John Schlesinger and Ken Russell made so many wonderful short films. And later I saw *Far from the Madding Crowd, Darling,* and in 1969 the hugely successful *Midnight Cowboy,* which established John as film director on both sides of the Atlantic, and won him an Oscar.

It was his great friend and casting director Noël Davis who booked me to do the choreography for John Schlesinger's *Yanks.* The film was to be shot mainly around Manchester, and so I made several visits up there to audition dancers before starting work. There was an important ballroom scene in the movie, during which a black GI is hauled off by the Military Police for dancing with a white girl. This so appalls the British girls that they dump their white partners and head for the black GIs: the kind of spirit that would appeal to John.

I started with a small group, and slowly worked up the numbers. On the day itself there were 700 extras. From time to time John would drop in to see how I was getting on. I very much wanted to please him.

Dining with Noël Davis one night on location, I said, "John seems so nice. He's always so appreciative of anything I show him."

"You wait," Noël said ominously. "He can go ballistic."

Only once or twice did I see this, and on each occasion it was with "the powers that be": the producers. To John, I learned, people in authority were there to help us. If they did their job, that was fine and normal; if they didn't, he'd let them know. Oh, yes!

He had little or no interest in power, and certainly none in those who sought it. As a colleague he was incredibly courteous. Should I – or any woman for that matter

– come to a meeting and find there was no chair, John would immediately give up his own, and go searching for another. And again, when we were working abroad, and he was invited to some party, he would insist that I and his assistant – usually Stephen Lawless – should also be invited. I never knew another director like this.

I always felt a good life-style mattered very much to John. It was as if his work fed his life-style and his life-style fed his work. He had his own chauffeur, a private secretary and houses in Kensington, Kent and Los Angeles, where he could entertain his friends and colleagues. John was very hospitable and seemed to accept very easily the good and the bad in all of us – especially in himself. I remember, when we were working at La Scala in Milan, Philip Langridge came to John for help, as he was finding the part of Peter Grimes difficult to play.

"He seems to care about Ellen and the boy, and yet he's hideously violent towards both of them."

"Yes," John said, "he's both. It's the way he is."

We next worked together in 1980 on *Les Contes d'Hoffmann* at the Royal Opera House in Covent Garden. It was John's first opera, and he approached the preparation as he might a film – with great attention to detail. A character was found for each member of the chorus, and the right costume matched to their photographs. Several weeks before rehearsals were due to begin he and I would spend each day in front of a model of the set, mapping out every move, tape recorder to hand and scores on our laps.

"No, I don't like that idea," John might say to me. "Think of another."

There were times when I wanted to say, "Hey, aren't *you* going to come up with something?" But I soon learned that like most film directors he expected others to come up with the goods. He would then use his considerable skill and discernment in knowing how to make best use of what was provided.

Curiously, though, when it came to rehearsals, John was petrified. Opera rehearsals can be rather alarming – there are so many people, from music department to stage-management, watching every move, with various scribes noting it all down. We all waited for John to begin, but he just sat there.

"Quick – get up and do something brilliant!" he whispered to me.

I've had some strange directives in my life, but this was certainly the most frightening. But thanks to our long preparation period, I was able to get things going.

After three days, John's assistant Richard Gregson asked me to give him a lift home.

"Is he ever going to do anything?" he asked me.

"I don't know," I replied.

But actually the three of us found a good way of working together, and once everything was placed, John would take over. The production was a big success; and is still in the Royal Opera House repertoire after three decades.

Later I worked with John on two of his movies – *The Innocents* and *Cold Comfort Farm* – and three further operas – *Der Rosenkavalier* at Covent Garden, *Ballo in*

Maschera at the Festspielehaus in Salzburg, and *Peter Grimes* at the Scala Milan and at the Dorothy Chandler Pavilion in Los Angeles.

(Hulton archive/getty images)
John Schlesinger on location in Florida, 1980.

We liked working together, and through the years became good friends – though to be honest, only to a point. I was always aware that John reserved his inner sanctum for his male friends. That was okay. One learns to have a certain delicacy in this area.

Underneath John's surface uncertainty, there was always a strong determination to get things right. The only thing that could get to him was if an artist started kicking up.

I watched this happen on two occasions – once with the Baron Ochs on *Rosenkavalier* because we had ignored his favourite piece of traditional business, and – again in *Rosenkavalier* – in the famous trio, this time with Kiri te Kanawa, Agnes Baltsa and Barbara Bonney. All three refused to take a step forward at a certain point as though joining the Music of the Spheres. John just stood there like a tank while the divas shouted at him. He was far too polite to retaliate. He waited until they had calmed down, turned, and with a crumpled face said to me, "They don't like what we're doing, Fiz!" (Gee, thanks, John!) We gave in of course, but were sorry to do so. Our maestro Georg Solti sat silently smiling. (As long as the music is fine...) There is a lot of traditional business in *Rosenkavalier*, which neither I nor John knew anything about. I'm happy to say the critic Bernard Levin wrote what a relief it was that John had got rid of it!

In 1989 we were to work together on *Ballo in Maschera* at the Festspielhaus in Salzburg. Placido Domingo was Gustavus, with Josephine Barstow as Amelia, and Leo Nucci and Sumi Jo as Renato and Oscar. The great Herbert von Karajan was to conduct. He must have been around eighty at this time; and he had not been well. Since they thought this would be his last production, money would not be a problem; – such was the esteem in which the Maestro was held. The designers sensibly took full advantage of this, and Bill Dudley's set and Luciana Arrighi's costumes were magnificent.

Before rehearsals began, John had been twice to Salzburg for preparation. On the second visit I went too, to audition the dancers. I much looked forward to meeting our famous Maestro. It was said of him that he was "a genius who painted with music" – a notion that appealed to me. Also that he loved beauty – "the beauty of sound, the beauty of music, the beauty of women, and the beauty of staging."

After my auditions, I went to join John while he lit the graveyard scene – one that takes place by night. Suddenly all the lights went on. "What the — ?" John blurted out.

The lighting designer explained that this always happened when the Maestro arrived – and that the lights would stay on until such time as Herr von Karajan was where he wanted to be.

A door at the back of the stalls flew open, and a minion of the administration called over, "Frau Fazan, Frau Fazan, come quick! The Maestro would like to meet you."

I was rushed to a corridor that stretched the full length of the enormous building. There were people lined up on either side. Herbert von Karajan, a frail creature with a beefy attendant beside him and an entire entourage, proceeded slowly down the line. It seemed we had been transported to the Middle Ages. When the great man stopped to be introduced to me, I very nearly fell to my knees; but managed somehow, with a bowing of the head, to exchange a few words.

I had been told that in Berlin the Maestro von Karajan had hailed a taxi. When the driver asked him where he wished to go, he replied, "It doesn't matter; I am wanted everywhere."

(photo by Margrit Munster)

Maestro Herbert von Karajan directing "Ballo in Maschera" 1989.

That night we went to a concert conducted by the Maestro. He was carried onto the podium by his strong and devoted attendant. He stood there in a black suit and trainers, his white hair brushed back; and with his chiselled rather beautiful profile, there was no doubt of his star quality. The violinist Sophie van Otta stood at the side of the podium, and their mutual support sent the music soaring.

Some weeks later rehearsals began. Each day the Maestro would be carried to a seat at the back of the stalls, with a microphone placed in his hand. Occasionally there would be a loud "STOP!"(which sounded in his accent like "TOPP!") – and we'd freeze. The Maestro would then give his notes, and we'd continue our work.

Everyone wondered how he and John would hit it off. Von Karajan was well known for having furthered his career in the 30s by joining the Nazi party. Both men were stars in their own spheres, and both enjoyed a grand lifestyle. Funnily enough, what seemed to draw them together was their sense of humour, a rather camp sense of humour on both sides. During a break in rehearsal, the adorable Josephine Barstow, who worshiped von Karajan, handed him a pile of photographs of the horses on her farm. Josephine was the tall, svelte English soprano whose loyalty to the English National Opera had won her great admiration.

"Eet ees no vonder she looks like a horse!" he whispered to John, and they both giggled.

At another break I heard him saying, "I don't understand you, John. All this Parliament! – all these people vorking around you! – I do everyting myself."

"Perhaps, Maestro, you're more clever than I am," John said.

"That ees very possible," said the Maestro; and they both laughed.

One night John was invited back to his home to view the rushes of a film von Karajan was making about himself. When I asked John the next day what it was like, he replied, "The whole thing was in close-up. Finally I did screw up the courage to suggest *one* long shot – of the orchestra. But I didn't get much response."

The Maestro was sometimes quite fierce at his own music calls. "Sit down, Placido!" he said crossly, as he rehearsed the duet in Act II. And one could feel his almost sensual pleasure in the soaring notes of the soprano Sumi Jo. It was as though nothing else mattered but the perfection of the notes. A far cry from London's Royal Court Theatre, where "perfection" was *not* a goal, and where the "Right to Fail" was a firmly held belief. Another world!

One day, working on stage, I was surprised to get a tap on the shoulder. Turning round I saw the Maestro's big tall attendant.

"Frau Fazan, the Maestro wishes to speak with you." I dropped everything and followed him through the pass door to where the great man sat at the back of the stalls, microphone in hand.

"I have been vatching you," he said. "You are not – how shall I put it?– " I held my breath. "You are not *maladroite*. I shall need your help when I take over next week. In this scene there must be no noise from the staircase. Not a sound. Can I rely on you?"

"Of course, Maestro." I don't like to think that I would have agreed to *anything* this charismatic man would have asked me – but... I floated back to work, taking care not to ruin my image by falling flat on my face.

Sadly, working together was not to be. On the Sunday evening that summer of 1989, John and I arranged to meet up at the theatre to go through the following week's schedule. As we arrived people ran out to meet us. We were told that our Maestro, the great Herbert von Karajan, had died that morning. It was a tremendous shock. John asked me to go to Josephine while he went to the administration. Josephine was inconsolable. Von Karajan, despite his cruel jokes, had been an ardent admirer of her talent, and instrumental in promoting her career.

The whole city of Salzburg lowered its lights and closed its doors in von Karajan's honour. Rehearsals were stopped. John was furious. He knew it was a good production, and felt we could go forward with the Maestro's assistant. The Festspielhaus wanted only the best to take over. And, luckily for us all, Georg Solti agreed to fill the gap.

When he arrived we ran the show for him, and he told us all that he had not wanted to accept at such short notice; but now that he had seen the production he was very glad that he had. Everyone was delighted. And indeed John's production was a huge success.

On the 23rd of July we attended a Requiem for von Karajan at Salzburg's Cathedral. Franz Kardinal König Altersbischof from Vienna officiated at the service. The Vienna Philharmonic played Mozart's *Requiem* with Ricardo Muti conducting. The chorus was from the Vienna State Opera, and the soloists were Ama Timowa-Sinow, Agnes Baltsa, Gosra Winbagh and Ferruccio Furlanetto. I sat between John and the costume designer Luciana Arrighi, who as a Catholic had come covered in black lace. This irritated John. "So stupid!" he whispered to me. She actually looked beautiful, but to John it seemed inappropriate, as if she were courting attention.

On the day after the general rehearsal, Bill Dudley, his wife, Stephen Lawless and I decided to take the lift to the top of the mountain behind the Festspielhaus, which is in fact built into the side of the mountain. We hoped to visit the Maestro's grave and pay our respects. Unfortunately, it was a horrid day. Clouds had settled on the top, and we could barely see five yards ahead. Ravens were flying and skulking around. I picked a few wild flowers and we went searching for the grave. We finally found it. It was on the edge of the cliff overlooking the city, surrounded by those Viennese flower baskets with huge round handles and bows – the sort you might see in an old Richard Tauber movie. The flowers had wilted and were mostly dead, the bows limp and bedraggled. It was a dismal sight. We all felt a little forlorn as we descended through the clouds to face our opening night in the theatre that had revered von Karajan so much.

Ballo in Maschera was a big success for all concerned, particularly for John.

My last production with John Schlesinger was *Peter Grimes*, in the year 2000. We opened in May at the beautiful Scala, Milan, and then at the Dorothy Chandler Pavillion in Los Angeles – a joint production for the two houses. But despite the beauty of the Scala and its wonderful work force, it was a difficult time, because John was not well. The poor reception of his 1998 film *The Next Best Thing*, with Rupert Everett and Madonna, was a blow – mostly, he told me, because he himself had thought that it was good. He lost faith in his own judgement, and became seriously ill. A heart attack led to a triple by-pass. The film had opened to bad notices, but what troubled John was that neither Rupert Everett nor Madonna had made any attempt to keep in touch with him while he was in hospital. That really hurt.

We started work on *Peter Grimes* far too soon after his operation. We prepared as we always had done, sitting in front of the model, tape recorder to hand and with little figures to move around. "Think of something good here," he'd say. But often after showing him something I'd turn round to find him asleep, his head drooped on his chest, and the score slipping to the floor. Not even the beauty of the Scala's auditorium or the big indoor courtyard of the stage-door, not even the skill of the backstage staff, could lift his spirit.

Happily, by the time we got to Los Angeles he was much better, though still not really himself. Placido as Artistic Director flew from New York to be there for the opening night. At the party afterwards he gave the traditional speech, thanking all and sundry; but he saved John for the last – a place usually reserved for the conductor.

"Whatever you want to do, John, whenever you want us to come – we will be here for you." Words to that effect. I was so pleased for John, because it had been a hard haul. He and I walked back to the apartment block together. He asked me to his house in Palm Springs to stay a few days with him and his partner, Michael Childers, but I had to get back to London.

"Call me before you leave," John said, and I did.

"I bet you slept well last night, didn't you, John?"

"No," he replied. "I was too excited."

He wrote to me from Palm Springs, telling me he'd been to check out a performance, and it was "wonderful and greatly appreciated." Also that he had been in New York for a showing of his film *Billy Liar*, which went really well – "Better notices than originally, I think, and it's getting well talked about. So I am holding my head up high again." This was October 2000.

Not long afterwards, on New Year's Day 2001, John had a very severe stroke. His partner Michael Childers made sure of his every comfort, and friends rallied round. Stephen Lawless phoned me from California to say that he'd been to see John in Palm Springs. He said that once you'd got used to the fact that the jolly Father Christmas we knew had turned into a little shriveled gnome, you could still have fun. "In fact as I arrived John said, 'Why, it's Lilly Law!'"

Sadly John was never able to return to England. His friends there missed him very much – his warmth and his humour. (As for missing his skill and talent – that went without saying.) For myself – and this may sound daft – I missed his extreme good manners. One only had to leave a box of sweets in his office to get a letter of thanks the next day. And every time we worked together there was always a generous letter of appreciation, often including a cheque with (and I quote) "I know how mean the Garden is towards you ..." or "Please don't push me away for this small token ..." Courteous to the end, his last words to Michael were, very typically, "Thank you."

22

PULCHINELLA:
STEPHEN FREARS

(photo by Sophie Baker)

Stephen Frears, 2004.

When Stuart Burge was the artistic director at the Nottingham Playhouse he quite often used to ask me up there to work on a production – among them Shakespeare's *King John*, Wederkind's *Lulu*, and Peter Barnes's *The Ruling Class*. I would stay with Stuart in the large house that the Playhouse reserved for visiting directors and choreographers. One morning at breakfast when I was up there working on *Rosencrantz and Guildenstern* the director Peter Wood declared,

"Stuart, the shower is not working. You'll have to call in Santa Fe." Stuart disappeared to the telephone in the hallway, returning to announce that Santa Fe was on his way.

True to his word he arrived, cheerily waving a spanner in one hand, with a bag of tools in the other. He was wearing a dark blue boiler suit and an American baseball cap – hence, I supposed, the name Santa Fe.

Later that night I asked Stuart if the plumber had done his stuff. Stuart laughed. "You mustn't be taken in by appearances," he said. "That's just a cover-up. He's actually a doctor, and pretty well off. He owns this large house and garden, as well as the large house and garden next door, where he lives with his family."

I don't actually remember when it was that I was told that Santa Fe was the father of the film director Stephen Frears. It doesn't matter, because for a long time now I have thought of Stephen as family. I first met him when he was assisting Lindsay Anderson at the Royal Court Theatre, and later Lindsay would take me to some of Stephen's film productions. My son Nicolas had worked as

Stephen's assistant director on music videos; and Stanley had written the score for three of Stephen's films – *My Beautiful Launderette, Sammy and Rosie Get Laid,* and *Prick up Your Ears.* On the tenth anniversary of Stanley's death Nicolas put some champagne in the fridge, and invited some of Stanley's old friends round for a drink. Only four people turned up. But Stephen was one of them. One doesn't forget things like that.

There is something lovable about Stephen. And yet... and yet I don't really feel I know him at all. Nor, it seems, do others. It's as if he hides himself behind a mask.

In a way I think of Stephen as the reincarnation of a *Commedia del' Arte* artist. After all, like Stephen those sixteenth- and seventeenth-century performers could take a story and turn it into a fascinating and relevant drama, because – again like Stephen – they knew how to "see clearly and unashamedly the life of their day." Stephen is well known for his ability to tap into the zeitgeist. Like Pulcinella, "that rogue of ingenuity," he uses this quality and allows it to inform all his work.

Even the way Stephen dresses is pure *Commedia del'Arte*: the tousled dark hair, the crumpled white linen suit and trainers, the mournful Pierrot expression and the soft baggy trousers for work.

For interviews about his own work Stephen's mask is firmly held in place. He dodges questions with replies like: "I've no idea," "Well, that's just the way it worked out," "Why don't you ask the writer?" Or, "Can I leave now?" Some people are charmed by the humility, others find it infuriatingly British. I'm left wanting more.

I had an opportunity to watch Stephen at work when in 2004 I choreographed the numbers of Stephen's film *Mrs Henderson Presents*. I noticed that he too directs as other film directors seem to. He waited to see what his team came up with. It was almost as if he felt any direction from himself might be an intrusion; even as a block or a barrier to someone's creativity. But I wasn't fooled. Stephen knows exactly how to deal with it – all of it. How long to hold a close-up, when to linger on a long shot, and exactly the moment to cut away. He once said to me, "If I get into one of your numbers, I won't be able to get out." Film has a language all of its own, and it's his.

Recently I saw Stephen being interviewed on television, first about the film directors he admired, and later about Tony Hancock and clowns. He was animated, very astute, and wonderfully articulate. Again I was reminded of his sixteenth-century *Commedia del'Arte* kindred, of whom it was written: "They had to be quick-witted, tough and adaptable or they perished. They felt out their way using whatever talent and luck they had, and they found the risk stimulating."

Privately, though, I think of Stephen as a wonderfully kind-hearted man who sees through his lens darkly. A curious antithesis which can't be very comfortable, but it works, and often brilliantly.

23

CURTAIN:
LAURENCE OLIVIER,
REBELS AND POETS

I'm old now. I'm not the person I was. I've reached the age when people talk across me, as though I didn't exist. There are times when I want to say, "Hey, just a minute! – You might learn a thing or two from me!" Curiously they don't seem to think so. But that's okay. I know how to keep on dancing. I only have to think of the last time I worked with Laurence Olivier.

It was on a Granada TV series in 1985, *Lost Empires*. Olivier was playing an old Variety artist well past his sell-by date, and it was my job with the musical director Joseph Ward to devise and rehearse all the various Variety acts; – Olivier's act to be somewhat tragical.

Joe and I worked out a routine for him that involved a funny song, a trombone, and some tacky jokes which I had got off the musicians. Laurence Olivier, we were told, had been through a lot of illness and had lost his short-term memory. I was warned that although I had worked with him before (when he started the Festival Theatre at Chichester, and on the movie *Oh What a Lovely War*), he would not recognize me. We weren't sure what to expect; so at our first meeting we were very polite and strictly professional. We played him the song, which seemed to please him, and he liked the idea of the trombone and the tacky jokes. These were the two he liked best:

(After a blast of the trombone): "That may not sound very good to you, but in five minutes the place will be full of Vikings."

And the other, after another blast: "Some people play for money – not me – I do it for spite."

After arranging rehearsal times, Joe and I quietly took our leave. When we were at the door Larry called out, "Goodnight, Fiz!"

"He recognizes you," Joe said, and we jumped up and down in the corridor. From then on we felt we could be less formal, and indeed rehearsals went well, and we rehearsed and fixed the whole thing.

The following week, while we were shooting the magician's act at the Grand Theatre in Blackpool, Larry's nurse called me over to where Larry was sitting watching in the stalls. He looked and sounded absolutely petrified. "You and I have a lot of work to do before the show tomorrow." My heart went to my boots. I realized he couldn't remember a thing about the act we had so carefully rehearsed together. We quickly fixed up a call and of course it all came back – including his bravado! When the producer and director came to tell us the time of the shoot, Larry said in a loud voice as they moved away – loud enough for them to overhear, "Who were *they*?!"

Laurence Olivier with Fiz and Soprano Jane Eaglen at Joseph Ward's party 1985.

Shooting the act wasn't plain sailing for anyone. Larry had asked me to walk up and down behind the camera to remind him of his moves, but it proved distracting. Cabbages and tomatoes had to be thrown at him. He looked frail and bewildered, as of course the character had to be. Even so ... I was glad when it was all over.

The next day Joe invited us to dinner at his house. I travelled there with Larry and his nurse in a taxi. He was in fighting form, pointing out various places where he'd been as a young juvenile lead. Knowing he'd felt none too happy the day before, I asked him why he still put himself through the hell of it all.

"It gets me away from Joan and the children," he joked. "Gives them a break!"

Clearly the trials of yesterday had gone; been pushed away – over – for after dinner he sat at the piano and gave us his party piece, "I'm only a Gigolo!" – word perfect!

He, the Lord Olivier of Brighton, then approaching his eightieth year, had us all falling about laughing. As someone said — You can't put your finger on greatness, but you know it when you see it. You could see the rebel in this great man – oh yes! And the guts. Perhaps you can't have one without the other.

I suppose I have always been drawn towards those who needed to kick up; those who couldn't just toe the party line; who wanted to change things for the better while knowing in their hearts that nothing really ever changes: the truth seekers, the outsiders.

Even then there are certain other heroes of mine who also fit the bill: the directors Elijah Moshinsky and Toby Robertson, for example; the intent but retiring producer Michael Codron, and the sensitive and wily writer/composer Lionel Bart.

My women friends – some of them very brilliant artists – were all performers. That's very different from working behind the scenes as I did; and I could never do them justice.

It annoys me sometimes that we are all creatures of our time, but I'm afraid we are. For instance, I showed a young woman my piece on George Formby. When she reached the part where he has got me up against the wall, she said, "Why didn't you give him a knee jerk? *I* would have!" and we both laughed.

"You are shameless," I said. "I wouldn't have dared. I'm very glad they're now bringing in all those rules against male abuse and harassment, for by the sound of it you're going to need them!"

"And you," she said, pointing her finger at me, "are shameful. You let them get away with it."

Did I? Probably I did. Well, I liked them. All those poets and rebels who flourish so well in our profession – I really liked them.

It would be presumptuous and somehow ridiculous for me to end now by quoting Shakespeare. And yet the Bard's thoughts on what a poet does would seem so very appropriate, albeit in my own paraphrase: "As the poet's eye wanders from earth to heaven and from heaven back to earth, his imagination conjures up things unknown, to which he will give a shape, and a place, making them real." This is what we all aspire to.

The other night my granddaughters Ellie and Anna Myers called round. Anna had recently had one of her poems printed in the school magazine, so I thought it might interest her to hear Shakespeare's description of the poet in *A Midsummer Night's Dream*.

"Hm," she said. "I'll have to think about that, Gran."

They were more interested in telling me about a film they'd seen – *District Nine*. I gathered there was a large band of aliens known as "Prawns," and a human goes to help one of them, only to find *himself* turning into a "Prawn."

"It was so sad," Anna said. "He finds a photograph of his wife, and wants to send her some flowers..." She choked, unable to go on. Ellie's big eyes filled with tears.

And I, who have lived in the realist humanist school, found myself thinking, Hey! The young may no longer look from earth to heaven and from heaven back to earth, but rather from screen to screen, and Facebook to Google, but they still have the imagination to give a shape to things unknown, even "Prawns." They "give to airy nothing / A local habitation and a name."

If I stick around I might learn a thing or two from *them*.

Lightning Source UK Ltd.
Milton Keynes UK
UKOW04f2349230913

217777UK00001B/78/P